Accelerate

A SKILLS-BASED
SHORT COURSE

ADVANCED

Series editor: Philip Prowse

SARAH SCOTT-MALDEN · JUDITH WILSON

MACMILLAN
HEINEMANN
English Language Teaching

Macmillan Heinemann English Language Teaching

Between Towns Road, Oxford OX4 3PP, UK

A division of Macmillan Publishers Limited

ISBN 0 435 28275 1

First published 1997

Designed by Ken Vail Graphic Design
Cover design by Threefold Design
Cover photograph by Frank Orel/Tony Stone Images

Illustrated by Archer Art (Ross), Paul Collicutt, Richard Dusczcak, Simon Girling and Associates (Alex Pang), Tony Randall, Martin Sanders

Photographs by: Jason Bell p11; Harry Borden p43; Bridgeman Art Library p25(b); Colorific p27(b); Environmental Images p60; Ronald Grant Archive p18; Impact p58(bl), 59; Kenji Kawakami/Chindogu Academy p48; The Kobal Collection p53; Thomas Hopker/Magnum p27(t), Martin Parr/Magnum p40; The Marsden Archive p46, 47; Pictor p18(bl), 26(b); Rex Features p20/21, 36, 37, 62, 89; Tony Stone p6(m), 58(t,mr,br), 59; Trip p26(a); Van Gogh Museum p25(t); Zefa p6(l), 18(br), 26(c).

Commissioned photography by: Sue Baker p38; Paul Freestone p6(r); Chris Honeywell p44, 61.

The series editor and authors would like to thank Catherine Smith, Claire Thacker and Celia Bingham for their professionalism, dedication and good humour.

The authors would like to thank Jane Henfrey and Sue Watson.

The publishers would like to thank Melrose Fernandes

Printed in Thailand
2005 2004 2003 2002 2001
13 12 11 10 9 8 7 6 5 4

The authors and the publishers would like to thank the following for permission to reproduce their material: Kate Adie for extracts from 'Non-Stop News' (The Listener, 21 October 1989); Daily Mail/Solo Syndication for extracts from 'The softer side of Joan Armour-plating' by Corinna Honan (25 August 1992); Evening Standard/Solo Syndication for 'Mum's the word' by Patrick McGowan (12 August 1996); Faber & Faber Ltd for extract from 'Justine' by Lawrence Durrell (1957); The Harvill Press for extract from 'Miss Smilla's feeling for snow'. First published in Danish by Munksgaard/Rosinante 1992, in Great Britain by Harvill 1993. Copyright © Peter Hoeg and Munksgaard/Rosinante 1992, in the English translation Farrar Straus & Giroux and The Harvill Press; Kenji Kawakami for extracts from 'Unuseless Japanese Inventions' (HarperCollins Publishers); Kodansha International Ltd for 'Stretched out' by Ishikawa Takuboku, translated by Carl Sesar from 'Takuboru: Poems to Eat.' English translation copyright © 1966 Kodansha International Ltd; Simon Marsden for extracts from 'The Journal of a Ghosthunter (Little, Brown UK, 1994); New Scientist for extract from 'The future of work' by Charles Arthure (16 April 1994); New York Times for extracts from 'Stop, Thief! And Give Me Back My Name' by Marcia Vickers (28 January 1996); The Observer for extracts from 'Mother's mad about the Internuts' by Carol Sarler (10 November 1995), and 'The happiest daze of Dreamtime' by Richard Neville (9 March 1996); Laurence Pollinger Ltd and the Estate of Frieda Lawrence Ravagli for extract of a letter from D H Lawrence to Edward Garnett dated 30 September 1913 from 'The Letters of D H Lawrence: Vol 2' (Cambridge University Press); The Rough Guides for extracts from 'The Rough Guide to Turkey' by Ayliffe et al and 'The Rough Guide to California' by Bosley et al; Kate Saunders/Options/ Robert Harding Syndication for extracts from 'Future shocks' by Kate Saunders (Options Magazine, 4/1994); Smash Hits for review of 'The Net' by Anita Naik (27 September–10 October 1995); Times Newspapers Ltd for extracts (adapted) from 'I am feeling fine, says woman who was pronounced dead' by Tim Jones and Joanna Bale' (The Times, 11 January 1996); The uninvited guest' by Marcelle Katz (The Sunday Times, 3 December 1995); 'Kitchen sink dramas' by Roland White (The Sunday Times, 14 January 1996); 'The wizard of oars' by David James Smith (The Sunday Times, 23 June 1996); 'Free for all?' by Christopher Middleton (The Sunday Times, 8 January 1996); and 'Language dies with tribal elder' (The Times, 15 January 1996); Walker Books for extract from 'The Tough Princess', text copyright © 1992 Martin Waddell. Illustrated by Patrick Benson; A P Watt Ltd on behalf of Michael Yeats for extract from 'When you are old and grey and full of sleep' by W B Yeats; The Watts Publishing Group for 'Tortoise's Big Idea' (pp 34–37 and illustrations pp 34 and 74) from 'The Orchard Book of Creation Stories' written by Margaret Mayo and illustrated by Louise Brierly, first published in the UK, by Orchard Books, a division of the Watts Publishing Group, 96 Leonard Street, London EC2A 4RH.

Contents

Map of the book

	Language focus	Skills focus
Unit 1 *No man is an island*		
Lesson 1 Private faces and public places Finding out about one another	Idioms with the word *name* Newspaper language	**Speaking:** giving personal information **Writing** a newspaper article
Lesson 2 Meet you on the Internet Relationships on the Internet	Reporting colloquial speech *Tend to* Words referring to insanity	**Reading** and reacting to an article **Speaking:** roleplay
Lesson 3 I ♥ Cliff A devoted pop fan	Telephone language Idioms and fixed comparisons	**Listening** to an interview for the main ideas
Unit 2 *Organise yourself*		
Lesson 1 The future of work The changing face of work	Imperatives with conditional meaning Superordinates	**Writing** a business scenario
Lesson 2 Finding time Managing your own time	Verb forms and future meanings Expressing purpose Fixed phrases with *time*	**Listening** to a lecture
Lesson 3 How to say no Saying what you mean	*No* and *not* Body language and idioms	**Speaking:** problem solving **Reading** for main ideas
Unit 3 *Bending the rules*		
Lesson 1 Marriage for ... ? Convincing the authorities	Inversion in conditional clauses *What if ... ?* *Get* Documents	**Writing:** building up a narrative
Lesson 2 The uninvited guest Getting in without a ticket	Linking adjectives together Compound adjectives Synonyms	**Reading** and reacting to a text **Listening** for detail
Lesson 3 Stop, thief! Return my name! Losing more than just a handbag	Clauses with present participles British and American English Money colloquialisms	**Reading** and **listening** for detail **Speaking:** roleplay
Unit 4 *Creating an image*		
Lesson 1 Artist's impression Appreciating pictures	Describing colour Literary language	**Speaking:** describing a painting in detail **Speaking:** discussing visual impressions
Lesson 2 Crowning glory? Hair and its significance	Lists in written text Vocabulary of hair and hairstyles	**Listening** for main idea
Lesson 3 He, she or they? Gender issues reflected in language	Clauses with present participle Fixed order idioms	**Speaking:** social and personal issues **Writing:** gender-specific language
Unit 5 *Another time, another place*		
Lesson 1 How it all began A traditional story about creation	Cleft sentences with *what* Verbs of movement	**Speaking:** telling a traditional story
Lesson 2 So far from home, so long ago An outside view of today's world	Present perfect for recent events Clauses with past participles Collocations	**Listening** to an extract from a novel read aloud **Speaking:** past and present events
Lesson 3 How do you say it? Pronunciation and regional accents	Pronunciation and spelling British and American pronunciation	**Speaking:** pronouncing difficult words

Lesson 1 *Private faces and public places*

Language focus: Idioms with the word *name*
Newspaper language

Skills focus: Speaking: giving personal information
Writing: recording information
from a conversation and writing a
newspaper article

1

Read the following phrases. They can all be completed with the same word. What is it?

1 He's always _____ -dropping.
2 That's my nick-_____.
3 Was that your maiden _____?
4 We're not really on first-_____ terms.
5 It rapidly became a household _____.
6 Don't call one another _____s.

2

Discuss what you think each of these people might be called. Use some of the names from the box below.

Colin	Corin	Corinne	Daughn	Dawn
Rebecca	Rebeca	Becca	Becky	Vaughan

3

Now listen and compare your answers.
What additional information did each person give to the interviewer?

4

Talk to your partner and ask questions to find out as much as you can about one another's names and their significance.

5

Write your partner's name at the top of a piece of paper and then summarise what you found out about them and their name. Display the papers around the walls.

6

Work with a new partner. Look at the topics below and talk for two minutes about Topic A. Then find your partner's paper and write what you have found out about them.

A an activity you really enjoy

Now do the same with topics B, C and D. Work with a new partner for each topic.

B a possession that you treasure
C one of your favourite places
D a person/people you are very fond of

7

Read what people have written about *you* and make any corrections or additions you feel are necessary. Then exchange papers with other students to find out about the class.

8

Make headlines from the following jumbled words.

HITS SPORTS BIG STUDENT STAR TIME THE

1 _____

FANS STUNS REVELATION LOVE

2 _____

HOLLYWOOD SETTING SPOT BEAUTY FILM TO BE LOCAL FOR

3 _____

Compare with a partner.
Which of the topics in Activity 6 could each headline relate to?

TURNS AFTER TREASURE LOST UP YEARS FIFTY

9

Work in pairs. Choose one of the headlines and write an imaginary story about some of the people in the class. When you have finished, find out how other students interpreted the headline you chose.

4 _____

_____

Homework

Take one of the papers from Activities 5–7 (either your own, or a friend's) and develop it into a fuller profile, correcting, editing and expanding where appropriate.

Language Summary

Idioms with the word *name*
  name-dropping

Newspaper language

see practice page 67

7

Lesson 2 *Meet you on the Internet*

Language focus:	Reporting colloquial speech *Tend to …* Words referring to insanity
Skills focus:	Reading and reacting to an article Speaking: roleplay

1

Have you ever:
– had a pen-friend?
– sent an e-mail message?
– used the Internet?

2

Look at this e-mail message and the reply.

> > Has anyone got any ideas on how
> to persuade your mum you've really
> grown up?
> > She's great but she won't let go…
>
> Same problem here – 90% of the time we
> get on fine then wham – feel like i'm
> 8 years old.

How would you reply to the message?

3

Look through part A of the text quickly and choose the sentence which best summarises it.

A mother
a is worried about the amount of time her daughter is spending using the Internet.
b describes how her relationship with her daughter has broken down because of the Internet.
c expresses her concern over her daughter's trust in relationships formed over the Internet.
d describes how she can no longer trust her daughter because of the Internet.

Part A

MOTHER'S MAD ABOUT THE INTERNUTS

Thought your kids were safe with Internet friends and cyberspace secrets? Wait for the doorbell …

Tap tap tappa tap-tap. It is the last sound to be heard before sleep. On especially bad days, it is the first sound to be heard in the morning. It is the sound of the only persistent disagreement in a household that is otherwise peaceful. My daughter is hooked on the Internet and I think that it is mad, bad and dangerous.

She is in every other respect a sensible young woman. She graduated in the summer, she goes to work each day, she and her friends monopolise the phone line each evening and she goes out with them at weekends. But on top of that she has lately started spending some two hours in intense communication with a computer. And I hate it.

This is not just technophobia. Of course, there is a value in instant access to information banks world-wide and, of course, e-mail is revolutionising the way we correspond with each other. My antipathy and mistrust are based upon the fact that this use of the Internet makes a mockery of the time-honoured way in which people communicate with each other. It leads to intimacy before acquaintance; it scatters secrets outwards, not inwards; and, most worrying of all, it is a vehicle for liars.

What frightens me is that my daughter rejects all this. The denial is there in the terminology she uses. "I 'met' Janet in January," she says, "and we've been 'friends' ever since". At other times, "I was 'talking' to Alex the other day and he 'said' …" "No, he didn't" I argue; friends are friends when, and only when, you have seen the whites of their eyes. She just rolls hers, skywards.

(The Observer)

---

hooked /hʊkt/ If you are **hooked** on something, you enjoy it so much that it takes up a lot of your interest and attention; an informal use.
nutter /nʌtə/ If you refer to someone as a **nutter**, you think that they are mad, or that their behaviour is very strange; used in informal British English.

4

Work with a partner. Student A should underline all the information given or implied about the mother in the text, and student B the daughter. What impression have you built up of the mother and daughter and their relationship?

5

Read part B of the text. What was the argument between the mother and daughter about? Who do you think won?

6

Continue to work with the same partner you had for Activity 4. Find as much information as possible about what your character (mother or daughter) said in the course of the argument.

7

Roleplay the argument, using the text as a basis.

8

In the text, the mother finds out that a similar situation is being used as an idea for a horror movie. In groups, discuss an outline for one possible plot, based on the main idea of the text. (It does not have to be exactly the same.) Think about how you would establish the main characters and situation, and build up tension to the climax. How would your film end?

9

Tell another group about your horror movie.

---

nerd /nɜːd/ If you say that someone is a **nerd**, you are saying in an unkind way that they are stupid or foolish, especially because they wear unstylish clothes and behave awkwardly in social situations; an informal word.

Homework

You are the daughter of the woman who wrote the article. Write an e-mail message to your friends on the Internet telling them about the argument with your mother and letting them know that the party is cancelled.

Part B

Imagine this. When I was planning to go away for a few days last month, this intelligent 22-year-old announced a plan for a party, the guests to include an assorted handful of Internuts who, coming as they would from all corners, would need to stay overnight.

Overnight? In my home, my home that contains everything I care about, rather high on the list being my daughter herself.

She said: 'Don't be silly.' She said it would be quite all right, because the people she was planning to invite were those whom she had 'known' for at least a year and whom she 'knows' as well as any of her other friends that, on the whole, I tend to like. I said, trying to be reasonable but not altogether succeeding, that in and among the things they 'tell' each other on the tap-tap, a tendency towards homicide might just have been overlooked, might it not?

The party did not happen. The row most certainly did.

When I say that if they are not nutters they are nerds, she tries for reason. Do I think she is a nerd? Absolutely not. Well, then, why should they be? Do I think she is a liar? Just as absolutely not. Well then.

But I cannot clear it from my head. It is not that, as individuals, I have reason to believe that they would lie. But they could. They could lie about their age, their sanity or even their sex. Indeed, apparently in America it is commonplace for men to tap-tap pretending to be women on the basis that they then get other women to communicate with far greater intimacy.

A thought occurs. The worst scenarios in my mind play like a horror movie. So I call a friend in Hollywood: has anyone thought of this for a movie plot? He laughs. There are five, to his knowledge alone, in development and one heading into production.

So now, I say to my daughter, we just wait for life to imitate art and we're home and dry. And murdered in our beds.

She laughs. 'See you in the morning, Mum. I'm just going upstairs to talk to my friends. Goodnight.' Tap tappa tap-tap …

(The Observer)

Language Summary

Reporting/colloquial speech
    She said **it would be** quite all right.

Tend to …
    … her friends, that on the whole I **tend to** like.

Words referring to insanity
    mad, bad and dangerous

see practice page 68

Lesson 3 I ♥ Cliff

Language focus:	Telephone language
	Idioms
	Fixed comparisons
Skills focus:	Listening to an interview for the main ideas

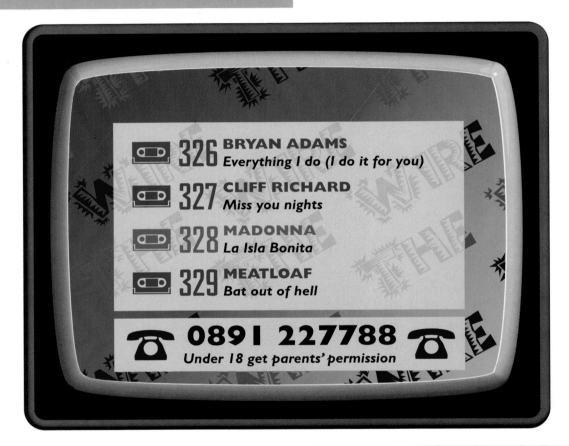

326 **BRYAN ADAMS** *Everything I do (I do it for you)*

327 **CLIFF RICHARD** *Miss you nights*

328 **MADONNA** *La Isla Bonita*

329 **MEATLOAF** *Bat out of hell*

☎ **0891 227788** ☎
Under 18 get parents' permission

1

Many cable TV companies have non-stop music channels which are interactive. The viewers control what is shown by phoning and requesting the videos they want to see.

Are there interactive TV channels in your country?

Have you ever phoned one?

2

You are thinking of requesting one of the videos on the list above. Listen to what happens when you dial the number, and answer the questions.

What should you do if …

1 you want to request video number 326 and you don't have a touch tone telephone?
2 you know the name of a video but you don't know the number?
3 you want to know which new videos have been released this week?
4 you have a touch tone telephone and you want to request a video?
5 you change your mind about the video you want half-way through phoning?

3

Would *you* request any of these four videos? Do you have a favourite pop video at the moment?

4

 Listen to Ken talking about his wife's favourite singer. Which video do you think she would choose from the selection on the TV screen opposite?

5

 Shirley's life has revolved around this singer for many years. Listen to Ken and makes notes on the ways in which Shirley shows her obsession.

Example She never misses a concert.

Homework

Write down five clues about a famous person you admire. Be ready to see if the class can guess who you have chosen in the next lesson.

6

Look at these expressions from the second listening passage. Decide if each expression refers to Ken, Shirley or the singer.

 1 shared our lives (*singer*)
 2 not jealous or resentful
 3 get teased a lot
 4 a really nice bloke
 5 like a member of the family
 6 helped the marriage survive
 7 caused some monumental rows …
 8 went absolutely spare
 9 put my foot down …
10 got the looks, the personality, the money and the voice …
11 be gone like a shot

 Now listen again and check.

7

Match each of these definitions to an expression in Activity 6.

a get very angry
b provoke huge arguments
c leave very quickly
d a very pleasant man
e refuse to allow something

8

What do you think about Ken's attitude to his wife's obsession? Would you behave in the same way as Ken?

9

Work with a partner. List all the products you (or your family) own that feature logos relating to music, film or sports stars (eg T-shirts, sweatshirts, baseball caps, bags, etc). Which are the most popular logos in the class?

Language Summary

Telephone language
   Hi. Thanks for **calling** the Wire.
Idioms
   I **put my foot down** about that.
Fixed comparisons
   She'd **be gone like a shot.**

see practice page 69

11

Lesson 1 *The future of work*

Language focus: Imperatives with conditional meaning
Superordinates

Skills focus: Writing a business scenario

1

Think of six jobs which are common nowadays. Now look at these illustrations and make a list of jobs that were common one hundred years ago and are not as common now.

2

Which do you think are the most common combinations of the words below?

1 neck	**a** letterheads
2 printed	**b** manager
3 scientific	**c** office
4 DNA	**d** journal
5 consumer	**e** massage
6 research and development	**f** day
7 division	**g** division
8 head	**h** products
9 working	**i** analysis

3

Work in three groups: A, B and C. You will hear three passages, each describing a modern business scenario. The three passages will be read twice, at normal speed.

Group A: Listen and make notes about passage A.
Group B: Listen and make notes about passage B.
Group C: Listen and make notes about passage C.

Then work with other students in your group to reconstruct the text you made notes on, trying to make it as close as possible to the original passage.

Everyone in the group should write out a copy of their final version.

4

Complete the appropriate column of the table below, using the text you wrote in Activity 3.

Next, make new groups. Each group should have someone with an A text, a B text and a C text. Each person in the new group should read out their text so that everyone in the group can complete the table.

	Text A	Text B	Text C
Product or service			
Office location/s			
Equipment/facilities used			

5

Which of the following areas of employment are disappearing (D), and which are expanding or likely to expand (E) in your country/countries? Discuss and write D or E next to each.

alarm and security equipment suppliers ☐

cable manufacturers ☐

career consultants ☐

childminders ☐

corporate hospitality organisers ☐

dictation and secretarial services ☐

factory cleaners ☐

hotel receptionists ☐

magazine layout artists ☐

introduction agencies ☐

photocopier suppliers ☐

sports equipment suppliers ☐

supermarket checkout staff ☐

trauma counsellors ☐

6

Listen to an expert on the changing nature of work in Europe and the US discussing the items from the list in Activity 5. Underline any items which he classifies differently from you.

7

Work in groups. Choose one of the following topics:

a medicine
b language learning
c housework
d sport

Discuss how this could be affected by changes in technology in the next few years.

Homework

Write an imaginary scenario similar to those in Activity 3 illustrating how the changes you discussed in Activity 7 might affect people or their way of life.

Language Summary

Imperative + *and/or* with conditional meaning
   Call it early in the mornng **and** you get an apologetic answering machine.

Superordinates
   A British consumer **products** company …

see practice page 70

13

Lesson 2 *Finding time*

Language focus:	Verb forms and future meaning
	Expressing purpose
	Fixed phrases with *time*
Skills focus:	Listening to a lecture

It's high time

Time's up

1

Work in groups. Complete the diagram on the right with phrases or idioms including the word *time* or *times*.

2

Listen to the speakers and add any new expressions including the word *time* to the diagram.

3

Do this quiz and find out where your time goes.

1 How much control do you feel you have in managing your time?
- **a** A lot of control ☐
- **b** An adequate amount ☐
- **c** Little control ☐
- **d** No control ☐

2 How do you use the hours of a normal weekday? Write how many hours you spend against each activity, to give a total of 24. Do the same for the weekend.

	Weekday	Weekend
a Sleeping	———	———
b Travelling	———	———
c Studying/working	———	———
d Eating	———	———
e Time with family	———	———
f Time to yourself	———	———
g Socialising with friends	———	———
h Housework	———	———

3 If you had more time outside work or school, how would you spend it? Tick as many as apply to you.
- **a** Time to yourself ☐
- **b** Time with your family ☐
- **c** Doing sport or exercising ☐
- **d** Social activities ☐

4 How often do you find yourself feeling short of time, on average?
- **a** Once a month ☐
- **b** Once a week ☐
- **c** Several times a week ☐
- **d** Every day ☐

4

Compare with another student. Can you draw any conclusions about your use of time?

5

Read about the problems three people had in coping with a writing assignment. What time management problems did each person have?

A

I found it hard to get started – I wasted quite a lot of time finding a decent pen, and sorting out my file. Once I got going I was OK – I had lots of ideas and notes and I knew what I wanted to say – but by the time I'd got half of it down on paper I was fed up with it, so I left the end until this morning and as usual the last part was rushed.

B

At first I tried to read everything I could find on the topic – that took ages and some of it was a waste of time. Then I couldn't think how to begin – or how to fit all the ideas together. I must have started it off at least five times. By midnight I had got into a real panic and ended up writing all night – but I don't think it's half as good as it could have been.

C

I planned it all out and wrote it … it took quite a long time because first of all my friend phoned up, then I stopped to watch something on TV, but in the end I thought it was OK but it was a bit untidy. So I started to write it out again – and then when I was half way through I changed my mind about the order but it'll have to do for the time being – I don't think I can face doing it again.

6

Now listen to an expert in time management discussing ways of using time effectively. List the ten techniques she describes.

1 *Keeping a time log* _____
2 _____
3 _____
4 _____
5 _____

6 _____
7 _____
8 _____
9 _____
10 _____

7

Which of these techniques would be of most use to each of the people in Activity 5? Are there any which could apply to your own situation?

Language Summary

Verb forms and future meaning
   I'm never **going to** get them finished in time.
Expressing purpose
   In order to plan ahead, you need to set goals.
Fixed phrases with *time*
   It's **high time** …

see practice page 71

Homework

Keep a time log for part of a day. Check the time at regular intervals (eg every 15 minutes) and note down exactly what you're doing (in English!). Bring your log to the next lesson to discuss.

Lesson 3 *How to say no*

Language focus:	*No* and *not*
	Body language and idioms
Skills focus:	Speaking: problem solving
	Reading: for main ideas

1

How many different ways can you think of to answer a Yes/No question without using 'Yes' or 'No'?

> Do you like the winter?

> I quite like it.

> Not much.

> I did last year.

> You must be joking!

2

Work in groups. Choose one person to answer questions. Ask him/her lots of yes/no questions as quickly as you can and see how long he/she can continue to answer without saying the words 'Yes' or 'No'.

3

Listen to these four conversations. What do they all have in common?

Discuss the situation in each case and suggest possible reasons why the person answered as they did.

Have you ever been in situations like this? How did you react and what did you say?

4

How could each person in the recorded conversations have said no? Choose one of the situations and write down exactly what you could say to refuse the request. Practise the dialogue with a partner and then perform it to the class.

5

The passage below is an extract from a magazine article. Read it and underline the main recommendations.

SAYING NO

When you say no you should do so promptly before the hopes of others are raised. Don't hum or haw or use terminology like 'I don't think so', 'It would be difficult right now', 'Maybe if …', 'I'll have to think about it', etc.
5 Such terminology creates a false sense of security and expectation in the other person and leads to resentment when you finally say no. In
10 addition to being prompt it is also important to be brief. People who go on and on weaken their position. 'Well I don't
15 really have much time  right now because I got caught up in this project I was asked to help out with and it really is time consuming.' Get straight to the point. 'No, I can't', 'No, it's not possible', 'No, it's not convenient'.

20   Shake your head when you say no as the combination of both verbal and body language is more powerful than verbal language alone. In fact communication experts tell us that words only communicate 10 per cent of meaning, tone of voice communicates 40 per cent and body
25 language the remaining 50 per cent. Don't smile when you say no as this may give a mixed message to the requester, and could also be interpreted as sarcasm.

    You should avoid giving long-winded apologies, excuses, elaborate explanations, justifications, etc. as these can
30 weaken your credibility and position. Avoid the word 'but'. This word imposes conditions and often causes the other person to become defensive. Use 'and' or 'however' instead.

    If softening of the refusal is required or the refusal is particularly difficult, perhaps because you are speaking to
35 a person in authority over you, you can use the sandwich technique. This entails using positives first (+), then the refusal (–), and then ending on a positive (+). An example of this technique is: 'I'm sure I would learn a lot by working on this project (+). However, I just don't have
40 the time right now (–). I think it's a great idea and I hope it works well for the department (+).'

    It is important to be calm, clear and concise. It is also important to be firm, direct and persistent – stick to your guns and only offer alternatives if you are sure you really
45 want to do them.

(The Executive Magazine)

6

Suggest alternative phrases with the same meaning for these expressions from the text.

1 hum or haw (line 2)
2 go on and on (lines 12–13)
3 long-winded apologies (line 28)
4 softening of the refusal (line 33)
5 stick to your guns (lines 43–44)

7

Look back at the dialogue you wrote in Activity 4. Does your refusal follow the advice given in the article? If not, change it and see whether it sounds more effective.
Would the advice in the reading passage be acceptable in your culture or would you need to change or add anything?

8

Read the following situations and discuss how you would say 'No' to each.

1 A stranger at an airport asks you to take a small parcel to someone in the country you are travelling to.

2 A group of overseas business representatives are visiting your company and want to see a presentation about your department. Your two colleagues have suggested that you give the presentation. You feel you always get asked to do this sort of thing and it is someone else's turn.

3 You have been working in the library all week reading and making notes to prepare for a test tomorrow. Another student who has done nothing all week asks to borrow your notes.

4 Your principal asks you to be on a committee to organise celebrations for the school's twentieth anniversary. You know that the committee will be meeting in the evening and the responsibility will involve a lot of extra work.

5 A relative asks you to look after their two-year old twins for the weekend.

6 Your neighbours ask you to look after their pets while they're away on holiday for three weeks. They've got three cats, two parrots, some very expensive tropical fish, a tortoise and a large fierce dog.

Homework

Choose one of the situations from Activity 8 (not number 1) and imagine that you have to reply in writing. Write a note or memo refusing the request.

Language Summary

No and *not*
  No, I can't!
  Do**n't** hum or haw.

Body language and idioms
  Shake your head when you say no.

see practice page 72

Lesson 1 *Marriage for …?*

Language focus:	Inversion in conditional clauses
	What if …?
	Get
	Documents
Skills focus:	Writing: building up a narrative

French man: You did it too.

American woman: Did what?

French man: Married me. I did it for the Green Card. What did you do it for? No one made you – no one.

1

What do you think these films have in common?
Have you seen either of them?
Why might people want to have a wife/husband from a particular country?

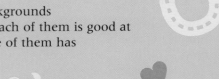

North Sydney NSW 20 years
Young guy seeks wife. Must be Australian.
Telephone 3130703 *for a hasty reply.*

2

Read this extract from a travel guide giving information about US immigration laws and answer the questions below.

In an effort to get round the stringent regulations on getting a social security number, more and more people are opting for **marriages of convenience**, usually on the basis of some kind of payment to the person willing to marry you. While such marriages are common, they're no guarantee of a **Green Card** (the cherished document that entitles you to legally live and work in the US). Indeed, the authorities treat all marriages involving foreigners with suspicion, and will interview you rigorously; should they suspect that your marriage is not legitimate, you qualify for immediate deportation.

(The Rough Guide: California and West Coast USA)

1 Why might US officials investigate marriages involving foreigners with particular care?
2 Do you know if your own country has similar regulations?
3 Do you know anyone who has changed their nationality? Why did they do it?
4 How would you feel about changing your nationality?

3

Work in groups of three or four students. You are going to write a story about the events before and after the marriage of these two people. First, decide on some background information. Discuss together and make notes about:

a their nationalities
b their names
c their family backgrounds
d one thing that each of them is good at
e a secret that one of them has

4

Your group can choose to write from the point of view of either the man or the woman. Choose one of these beginnings:

I woke up with the sun streaming through the curtains. I knew it was going to be a good day ...

Someone spoke to me. I turned round. It was a face I vaguely recognised.

I hadn't wanted to go to the party. But that afternoon ...

Discuss how the first paragraph will continue and make some notes.

5

Read the sentences below and opposite to give you some hints about how the story might develop. Decide together how your story continues. Use your own ideas and those suggested by the sentences. A possible structure could be:
– the meeting
– the negotiation and preparation
– the wedding
– a regret and a problem
– the ending
Think about the ending you want to give your story – happy, tragic or ambiguous?

I'd been something of a globetrotter and hadn't found a country I wanted to settle in until ...

I didn't want to make too much fuss but, after all, I was getting married. So I went out and bought ...

I thought I'd got to know him quite well but nothing could have prepared me for the proposition he made me ...

We went to great lengths to make the whole thing seem convincing. We took photographs ...

Homework

Design a video cover for the film of your story. Include information about the title, and actors, and write a summary of the film for the back cover (about 60 words). You can include a picture if you want.

6

Within your group, decide which part of the story each person is going to write.
Now write your own part of the story, liaising with your group to ensure that the story is consistent. You can include some of the sentences below if you want to.

7

Think about how you will present your story and find pictures to illustrate it if possible.

8

Read or listen to the stories of other groups in the class and decide whose story you think would make the best film. Who would you choose to star in it? What would you call it?

As the day approached, I began to feel nervous. What if we were found out? What would happen to me? What if I met someone else after the wedding? I forced myself not to think about it too deeply.

"I've decided I want to stay here. If we got married, I could. I'd pay you, of course."

That piece of paper seemed to be my passport to a new life ...

For a moment when I was saying my vows I felt a stab of regret – had this been someone I loved, I wouldn't ...

Language Summary

Inversion in conditional clauses
   ... should they suspect that your marriage is not legitimate ...

What if ...?
   What if we were found out?

Get
   In an effort to **get** round the stringent regulations ...

Documents
   ... the cherished **document** ...

see practice page 73

19

Lesson 2 *The uninvited guest*

Language focus:	Linking adjectives together Compound adjectives Synonyms
Skills focus:	Reading and reacting to a text Listening for detail

1

Discuss in groups. Have you ever been to any of the social events listed below? On what basis were you invited? (eg as a friend? through business contacts?) Tell your group about one of the events that you enjoyed. Are there any other types of events you have been invited to?

a birthday party	**a child's naming ceremony**
a film preview	**a graduation**
a cocktail party	**a wedding reception**
the launching of a new product	

2

Match a word from each list to make ten compound adjectives.

1	high	**a**	tingling
2	star	**b**	cut
3	high	**c**	spotted
4	gilt	**d**	edged
5	double	**e**	oiled
6	well	**f**	profile
7	high	**g**	breasted
8	well	**h**	society
9	red	**i**	studded
10	skin	**j**	powered

Now read the text opposite quickly and find the ten compound adjectives.

3

Read the text again to find the answer to the following questions.

1 What is unusual about what Claude Khazizian does? What is the word used to describe this activity?
2 What social events are mentioned in the article?

onsieur Claude, as he is affectionately known, is one of a rare breed: an eccentric Frenchman with Armenian blood in his veins. A bon viveur, a practical joker, who likes attending high-society galas and parties. 'So what,' he says. 'Wouldn't you?'

There is, however, just one snag: he is not usually invited to these events. And yet Claude Khazizian, 64, has become something of a society fixture. Bold-faced and bonily handsome, he has been pictured in glossy magazines with Queen Helena of Spain, Prince Joachim of Denmark, and the President of France. His next target? 'I don't like to plan too far ahead,' he claims, 'but I'd like to see the Queen of England.'

It all started when, some years ago, he was snapped with Sharon Stone at the Cannes Film Festival. A couple of months later in Paris, it was the supermodel Claudia Schiffer's turn. Then he was caught on camera behind François Mitterand and President Jacques Chirac. Later that month, the same smooth, suave face was seen bobbing between the Danish Royals at the wedding of their son.

At all such events, whether we are talking about a star-studded soirée or a high-powered political lunch, Khazizian is an affable and amusing guest. But he is also, much to the extreme irritation and misery of the attending security guards, uninvited. No gilt-edged card, no identity badge. Nothing. He pops up like a jack-in-the-box. Just who is this high-society gatecrasher?

'I am', he says, puffing out his expensive double-breasted charcoal jacket, 'merely an average middle-class Frenchman. Everyone asks me why I should attend exclusive functions. My short reply is: Why not?' Through a mixture of luck, well-oiled charm and sheer cheek, he has simply managed to slip through cracks in the heavy security at the high-profile events he attends. He has, he says, the ability to melt into a crowd. 'And when you're dealing with the human element,' he explains, 'there is always a weak link. A gap. A little smile and a joke, and you've already won half the battle.'

And if there's one thing Khazizian likes, it's a joke. We meet in a hotel near his home. In the quiet blandness of its lobby, he seduces everyone in his path with a set of neat, off-the-cuff quips. Propelling himself forward with an easy smile and well-cut suit, cherry tie and red spotted pocket handkerchief, his regal, beaky features give him the immediate appearance of being important.

Khazizian's wife, Simone, doesn't even like parties and his two children regard his behaviour as nutty and unnecessarily provocative. So why does he take the risk? It's pure, skin-tingling fun, that's why. 'What I'm doing is exercising my freedom and indulging in a bit of equality,' he says. 'From a street sweeper to a king, we're all just human beings. I just don't believe in barriers. I don't think what I'm doing is illegal.'

Smoothing an invisible crease out of his suit, he says, 'The tabloids have branded me an impostor. I would like to correct this. Remember, although I may be a gatecrasher, I have never pretended to be anyone other than myself.'

(The Sunday Times)

Homework

You are writing another article about gatecrashing for a magazine. Choose one of the speakers from Activity 5. Think about how you imagine this person and your attitude to their behaviour. Write two paragraphs describing the person and what they do.

4

Look at the text again and discuss the following questions with another student.

1 The social events Claude attends usually have heavy security. How does he avoid this?
2 How far do you think Claude's reasons for what he does are justified?
3 Do you agree with the tabloids' judgement on Claude? (last paragraph)
4 How would you react if he turned up at an event you had organised?
5 How would you describe the tone of this article? Is it mainly critical, admiring, amused or factual?

5

 Listen to three people talking about how they gatecrash social events and complete the table.

	Gatecrashing technique
Speaker 1: _fashion student_ Event: _____ _____	1 Showing _____ _____ 2 _____ loudly to person behind 3 Wearing lots of _____ . 4 Pretending you're with the _____
Speaker 2:_____ Events: _____ _____or _____	1 Stamping each others' _____ 2 Throwing _____ _____ to friends. 3 Wearing anorak with _____ _____ _____ 4 Following behind the _____
Speaker 3:_____ Event: _____	1 Hiding on _____ under _____ 2 Hiding under a _____ _____

6

Does gatecrashing happen in your country? If so, do people use the same techniques as the ones described in Activity 5?

Language Summary

Linking adjectives together
    ... Khazizian is an **affable and amusing** guest.

Compound adjectives
    No **gilt-edged** card ...

Synonyms
    ... he has been **pictured** ...

see practice page 74

Lesson 3 *Stop, thief! Return my name!*

Language focus:	Clauses with present participles British and American English Describing how much money someone has
Skills focus:	Reading and listening for detail Speaking: roleplay

1

Look at the picture for a minute then close your book.
Write down all the contents of the handbag. Compare
with a partner then open your book and check.

1 CASH
Thieves are usually not looking
for money, but it is a nice bonus.

2 PHONE CARD
Phone cards are usually very easy
to use and often do not even require
a personal identification number.

3 SOCIAL SECURITY CARD
With a social security number,
thieves can easily open new
charge accounts or checking
accounts that will allow them to
write bad checks.

4 CREDIT CARDS
Rather than risk charging
something on a stolen card that
may have been canceled, thieves
often prefer using the stolen cards
as the identification they need to
obtain new ones.

5 CHECKS
Even after a checking account has
been closed, a lot of places will
still unknowingly accept bad
checks from someone who can
show ID.

6 DRIVER'S LICENSE
Rather than risk using a stolen
license with the owner's
photograph, thieves sometimes
create a fake with their own
likeness, lifting details from the
stolen ID.

7 AUTOMATIC TELLER CARD
To use this a thief needs to
know the personal identification
number (PIN).

2

Some of the descriptions in the picture above are
incomplete. Complete them where necessary by adding
one or two of the sentences below.

a A common method is to pose as a bank representative,
call up and say the number is needed to expedite getting
a replacement card.

b Companies usually examine their records to determine
to what extent a customer is liable for disputed calls.

c Consumers are usually not liable for bad checks but
informing a bank quickly of lost or stolen checks can
limit the difficulty of disputing bad-check claims later.

d In some cases, stores will give thieves cash for
returned merchandise bought on their cards.

e Most thieves know they can get more money by
gaining access to credit or checking accounts.

f Or thieves will go through your belongings looking for a
birthday or address that might have been used as the PIN.

3

Discuss in groups. Have you or has someone you know
ever had anything stolen?
Imagine you discovered that your bag or jacket had just
been stolen:
– would you know exactly what was in it? For example,
do you know exactly how much money you are
carrying at present?
– would there be anything in your bag/jacket that a
thief could use? (eg keys)
– which object or objects would you be most
worried about?
– would you take any action, apart from informing
the police?

4

Marcia Vickers, a journalist who works in New York, was the victim of a theft. Read Marcia's account of the theft below and make notes to complete her statement for the police, giving as much detail as you can of exactly what was stolen.

My ordeal began when I was having a leisurely lunch with my editor at a restaurant in West 57th Street named – what else? – *Lucky's*. I reached down to retrieve my black leather bag from the floor. It was gone.

I felt sick. My life had been in that bag. My monetary loss was negligible, just $10 and some subway tokens. But the thief got not only a bunch of my credit cards and my bank card, but also my checkbook and Filofax, in which I keep my phone card, library card, address book – just about everything that defines me.

My editor and I hurried back to the office, where I immediately called and canceled my American Express, Visa, and store cards. But, having 15 cards in all, I was not exactly sure which had been stolen, because I kept some in my wallet, others in the back of my date book, and still more at home.

Next I dashed to the closest Chase Manhattan Bank branch, arriving minutes before it closed, and canceled my automatic teller machine card and checking account. My editor provided me with some cash, and I was off by taxi to my Upper East Side apartment. I knew there was no time to waste. Within an hour, a locksmith had changed the bolt lock on my door. Meanwhile, I took a better inventory of other cards that were stolen and called and canceled them. (This was one time when I could have used a credit card registry service, which, with one call from me, would have made all the notifications.)

I also called my parking garage, leaving instructions that under no circumstances should anyone but me be allowed to claim my car.

(The New York Times)

```
NEW YORK FEDERAL POLICE DEPARTMENT
NOTIFICATION OF THEFT STATEMENT:
Name _____
Telephone number  212-243-2874 _____
Time of incident _____
Place of incident _____
Full description of stolen article/s _____
```

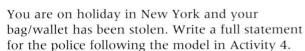

Homework

You are on holiday in New York and your bag/wallet has been stolen. Write a full statement for the police following the model in Activity 4.

5

Underline all the things Marcia did to try to limit the damage the thief or thieves could do.

6

Listen to what happened after the theft. Tick the things the thief or thieves did.

1 Tried to trick Marcia into giving her PIN number. ☐
2 Opened a charge account and bought three Armani sweaters. ☐
3 Changed the photo on her driver's licence. ☐
4 Used her identity card to open charge accounts. ☐
5 Bought six extra-large goose down jackets on her account. ☐
6 Tried to get money by returning the jackets and demanding a refund. ☐
7 Left threatening messages on her answerphone. ☐
8 Wrote checks and forged her signature. ☐
9 Opened new bank accounts in her name. ☐

7

Roleplay the following situation in pairs.

Student A: Imagine that 'the other' Marcia has been found. You are a social worker. Try to find out what her background is. Why did she start to steal? Did she actually steal Marcia's bag and if not, who did? Who was the man who rang Marcia the first night? What happened later – was she ever afraid of being caught? How did she eventually get caught? What does she think will happen next?

Student B: You are 'the other' Marcia. Reply to Student A's questions.

Language Summary

Clauses with present participles
But, **having fifteen cards in all,** I was not exactly sure …

British and American English: Spelling and vocabulary

Describing how much money someone has

see practice page 75

Lesson 1 *Artist's impression*

Language focus:	Describing colours
	Literary language
Skills focus:	Speaking: describing a painting in detail
	Speaking: asking and answering questions about visual impressions

1

How much do you know about colour? Try this quiz.

1 Chrome, primrose and saffron are all shades of one primary colour. What is the more common term used for this colour?

2 What are the names of the seven colours of the spectrum? Clue: their initial letters, in order, are R O Y G B I V

3 The precious stones lapis lazuli, sapphire and turquoise are all this colour.

4 What colour are the fingers of a good gardener? (Careful – this is an idiom!)

5 In a Hindu wedding, the bride wears this colour.

6 Complete these two idioms of colour:
a as _____ as a beetroot.
b as white as a _____ .

7 This is the colour of sadness and mourning in Islamic cultures.

8 In China this is a very lucky colour.

9 An object that absorbs all wavelengths of light will appear to be this colour.

10 'Carroty' and 'ginger' describe this colour of hair.

2

The words and expressions below all describe shades of brown.
a Which of them are related to food and drink and metals and jewels?

> **amber   beige   bronze   camel   chocolate brown**
> **coffee coloured   copper coloured   nut-brown**
> **tan   toffee coloured**

b Now use some of these words to describe the shades of brown in the pictures opposite.

3

Work in groups. Choose another colour, eg red, blue, green or yellow. Think of some ways of describing different shades of that colour and make a list of all the words you find. Try to find examples of as many of these shades as possible in the pictures or in the classroom. Then compare your list with another group who chose a different colour.

4

Which of the paintings do you prefer?
Discuss the similarities and differences in the subject matter and style of the two pictures.

5

The phrases below are taken from descriptions of the two pictures. Match each phrase to the picture it describes best.

1 … the red, pink and orange tones of the women's clothing …
2 … a small portrait image in the background …
3 … a chrome background scattered with childish flowers …
4 … the greenish-blue shadows …
5 … although the face reflects the colours that surround it, it stands out strikingly …
6 … the vivid colour combinations …
7 … balancing these hot hues against the cooler but nevertheless rich bands of colour in the landscape …
8 … the exaggerated angles of the face …
9 … the sculptural relation of the two figures …
10 … the colour is far from nature …
11 … very sad … the face of a man who is ill and tormented …
12 … huddled together and looking sideways across the canvas, they seem threatened and nervous …

Gauguin *Self-portrait 'Les misérables'*

6

Work with a partner. Choose one picture each. Think about the title, the story behind the picture, the overall impression and the details, the exact descriptions of colour, etc. Next, close your book and describe your picture from memory in as much detail as possible. Your partner (who can look at the picture) may ask you questions.

Homework

Write a paragraph describing a picture (real or imaginary). Describe the content, style and colours of the picture and discuss what it means to you and why you like it.

Language Summary

Describing colours
... the **greenish-blue** shadows ...

Literary language

see practice page 76

Gauguin *When will you marry?*

25

Lesson 2 *Crowning glory?*

Language focus:	Lists in written text
	Vocabulary of hair and hairstyles
	Pronunciation: stress and intonation
Skills focus:	Listening for main idea

1

Discuss in groups.
- What hairstyles are in fashion in your country at the moment?
- Do younger people have hairstyles which are different from those of the older generation?

2

Listen to four people describing themselves at the time the photos below were taken. Match each speaker with the correct photo and complete the table with the expressions they use to describe their hair at the time of the photo and at present.

	Picture	Hair then	Hair now
1			
2			
3			
4			

3

Discuss in groups.
1 Which of the hairstyles in the pictures below do you like/dislike?
2 Do you think any of these styles would be regarded unfavourably by:
- school authorities?
- an employer?
- a person of the opposite sex?
- an older person?
3 Is your hair very different now from when you were younger?

4

What sort of clothes would you expect each of the people in the photographs below to be wearing?

5

These paragraphs are extracts from an article about hair symbolism. Match each paragraph to a heading from the list.

1 An unrivalled feature
2 Rites of passage
3 Strength, length and life
4 Ornamentation or symbolism?
5 Marginal or controlled?
6 Witchcraft, death and worship?

A

In nearly every society of the world men and women af all ages spend a remarkable amount of time doing a variety of things to their hair – curling it and straightening it, plaiting it and bunching it, shaving it off and plastering it with mud, and even sacrificing it on altars. Some of these ways of treating hair are merely decorative, but others have a much deeper significance.

B

If the body is to be used for ritual purposes, the hair is the most obvious place to begin since, like the nails, hair grows continuously and can be cut without pain. But, unlike the nails, the hair of the head is suitable for dressing, plaiting and ornamentation. The relationship of hair to the body as a whole is also vitally important; the most prominent type of hair grows on the head, and the head itself has a special significance in symbolic thought.

C

The use of a person's hair for magical purposes is a custom found all over the world. Hair can be the means of conveying a supernatural force between man and man, as in the case of sorcery; between the living and the dead, as with mourning rites; or between men and gods, as with the sacrifice of hair on the altars of particular gods.

D

The hair, in comparison with every other part of the body including the nails, has extravagant powers of growth. This in itself is sufficient to make it an important symbol of power and vitality in many cultures.

E

The general theme is that long hair is associated with being outside society and that cutting the hair symbolises re-entering society or living under a particular disciplinary regime within society.

F

Another ritual associated with hair is the shaving of children's heads. In Cambodia, Thailand and Laos each child traditionally has the hair shaved in the first month after birth – 'cutting the wild hair' as it is called. After this the head is kept shorn (with the exception of a topknot) until the end of childhood, when the topknot is removed at the initiation and the entry into maturity.

6

Discuss in groups.
1 How many of the things you can do to your hair mentioned in paragraph A are common in your culture? How many of them have you done yourself?
2 Are the ideas in paragraph E true about your country now? Have they ever been in the past?
3 Are there any rituals involving hair connected with childhood or death in your own culture?

7

In groups decide on a typical hairstyle and three typical items of clothing for:
– a male of your own age
– a female of your own age
– a man of your father's age
– a woman of your mother's age
– a man of your grandfather's age
– a woman of your grandmother's age

Write a description of each one in as much detail as possible – style, colour and (for clothing) material and pattern.

8

Read out the descriptions from Activity 7 in jumbled order to someone from another group. Can they guess which age-group your description is of, and if it is a man or a woman you are describing?

Homework

Find an old photograph of yourself and write a short paragraph describing what you look like there and what you look like now. Include details of your hair and clothes.

Language Summary

Lists in written text
    ... suitable for **dressing, plaiting and ornamentation** ...

Vocabulary of hair and hairstyles
    I had my **hair bleached with streaks**.

Pronunciation: Stress and intonation

see practice page 77

Lesson 3 *He, she or they?*

Language focus:	Clauses with present participle Language and gender Fixed order idioms
Skills focus:	Speaking: discussing social and personal issues Writing: avoiding gender-specific language

1

Is it possible to tell a man from a woman by their reactions to everyday situations? Some psychologists think so. But how about you? Try this questionnaire!

The situations below have been identified as ones in which men and women may behave differently. Decide in each case which person is probably a man, and which a woman.

1 A couple are in a restaurant, looking at the menu.
a) Who chooses something they've never eaten before?
b) Who sticks to what they know they like?

2 A man and a woman are sitting next to one another on a seat with shared armrests.
a) Who has their elbows on both armrests?
b) Who keeps their elbows in by their sides?

3 A man and a woman are shopping for new clothes.
a) Who looks around at the selection available first?
b) Who asks the assistant for a particular style and colour straight away?

4 A man and a woman each select one from a box of chocolates.
a) Who takes a bite to see what's inside?
b) Who eats the whole chocolate at once?

5 A man and a woman both have several jobs to do in a fixed period of time.
a) Who does the jobs one by one, finishing one before beginning another?
b) Who prefers to work on several different jobs at the same time?

6 A couple are driving home. They notice the car is getting rather low on petrol.
a) Who wants to fill up at the next petrol station?
b) Who wants to risk it and get straight home?

7 A man and a woman are in a shop selling a range of home appliances.
a) Who heads for the display of new products?
b) Who looks at the familiar items?

8 Driving in a strange town, a couple realise they're lost.
a) Who would stop and ask for directions?
b) Who would keep driving until they found the way?

Compare your choices with the answers on page 66. Would the same distinctions apply in your own country? Can you think of any additional situations? If so, make additional questions for the quiz and try them out on other people in the class.

2

Read the following extract from a pamphlet of advice to writers. Do the problems it mentions occur in your language? Do you have different words for all these items?

Studies of native English-speaking college students and school children have shown that the generic use of *man* (ostensibly to include all humans) does not elicit mental images of both sexes. When told that 'man needs food and shelter to survive' the great majority of the people in the studies visualised only men. Foreign language learners who perceive the word *man* as a term for males will thus be echoing the feelings of native speakers. Building towards a native-like language competence will therefore mean avoiding the use of false generics in teaching materials – for example, instead of *mankind*, use *people*, *humans* or *humanity*, and instead of *manpower* use *staff* or *work force*. In the same way the false generic *he* and other masculine pronouns should be avoided as in 'A person generally learns what he uses and forgets what he doesn't use'. The problem of the generic *he* could be avoided by making the sentence plural – *People generally learn what they use …'* or sometimes by using the second person '*You generally learn what you use …'*. In other cases *they* may be used as a singular 'neutral' pronoun, eg '*Ask every student in the class what they want …'* (note that the verb is still plural)

3

Now look at the passages below. Underline the parts which could be criticised according to the criteria above. Then rewrite the passages to remove the problems.

A If a student wants to take advantage of the student discount card he should first bring a photocopy of his ID card to the office together with his completed application form to be signed by the headmaster. It will not be possible for anyone to use his card without a valid stamp and signature.

B The manpower required to keep a large factory functioning one hundred years ago was considerable. Machines were maintained and manned by an army of working men. Many men's jobs were dangerous and a man had little recourse if he was injured or maimed in the course of his work. There was always another man to fill his place.

Homework

Find six words which specifically refer to a male, eg *bachelor* and six words which specifically refer to a female, eg *wife*.

4

You are going to hear sixteen everyday words. As you hear each word, decide if your first association with that word is female or male. Write the word down under the appropriate heading.

Female	Male

Compare your answers with another student and discuss what may have influenced your choices.

5

Work in groups. Look at the following statements. Do you agree with them? If not how would you change them with reference both to English and to your own language?

1 In expressions like 'men and women' it's natural to put the man first.
2 In a list of people's names it's more polite to put a title (Mrs/Miss) in front of a woman's name whereas a man can be referred to by his name only.
3 In a conversation, men are much more likely to interrupt than women.
4 Women tend to use more emotive adjectives such as 'lovely'.
5 Men typically use less body language than women.
6 Men use more assertive intonation than women.
7 Insistence on the use of non-sexist language will eventually lead to a decline in sexist attitudes.

Show your results to someone from another group. How similar are the ideas of your two groups?

Language Summary

Clauses with present participle
   One listener agrees, **citing** opinion surveys.

Language and gender
   … instead of **mankind**, use **people** …

Fixed order idioms
   man and wife

see practice page 78

Lesson 1 *How it all began*

Language focus:	Cleft sentences with *what*
	Verbs of movement
	Pronunciation: weak forms,
	linking, elision
Skills focus:	Speaking: telling a traditional story

1

Think of some similarities and differences between a tortoise and a stone.

2

In this lesson you will read and hear a traditional African story. The story is about a tortoise and his wife, a man and a woman, and some stones. Complete the lines by adding the dialogue below.

- **a** A time will come when you must die.
- **b** First give us children.
- **c** I've been thinking.
- **d** If you have children, you can't live for ever.
- **e** Let's go and ask the Maker for some.
- **f** Mmmm … what you want is children.
- **g** Otherwise there will be too many tortoises.
- **h** Please give us some little tortoises.
- **i** So would I.
- **j** That is how it shall be.
- **k** That would make me very happy.
- **l** Then let us die.
- **m** Think carefully.
- **n** What I'd like most of all is to have lots of little tortoises.

 Now listen and check.

3

The next part of the story is about the man and woman. It is very similar to the first part. It begins:

> When the man saw all the little tortoise children toddling around, playing with their parents and having fun, he said to the woman …

In pairs, tell the next part of the story, following the language and pattern of the first part as closely as you can.

Tortoise's Big Idea

In the beginning, nothing ever died. The tortoise and his wife, and the man and the woman, the stones – everything there is – lived for ever. It was the Maker who arranged it that way.

But one day the tortoise said to his wife,

(**1**) '_____

(**2**) _____ ,

(**3**) '_____,' said his wife.

(**4**) '_____

(**5**) _____ '

    Off went the tortoise and his wife, *crawl, crawl.*

They came to where the Maker lived, and they said to him,

(**6**) '_____ ,

    (**7**) '_____,' said the Maker.

(**8**) '_____

(**9**) _____

(**10**) _____

(**11**) _____ ,

    And the tortoise and his wife said,

(**12**) '_____

(**13**) _____ ,

    (**14**) '_____,' said the Maker.

    The tortoise and his wife went home, *crawl, crawl.*

And soon – great joy! such great joy! There they were – lots of little tortoise children.

(The Orchard Book of Creation Stories)

4

The last part of the story is about the stones. Discuss with your partner how you think they relate to the theme of the story and think of a possible ending.

5

Work with two other students from different groups. Student A should retell the first part of the story (about the tortoises) from memory. Student B should tell the second part (about the man and woman). Student C should tell the third part of the story, with the ending prepared in Activity 4.

6

Listen to the last two parts of the story and compare them with your versions. Do you know any similar stories from your own country?

7

Look at the picture on the right and choose one of the following activities.
1 Think of a story or myth for the picture and prepare to tell it.
2 Imagine you are sitting with the people in the picture. Look around you and prepare to describe why you are there and what you can see.

8

Find another student and tell one another your stories.

Homework

Write out either the complete story of the 'Tortoise and the Stones' or your story from Activity 7.

Language Summary

Cleft sentences with *what*
　What you want **is** children.

Verbs of movement
　Off went the tortoise and his wife, **crawl, crawl.**

Pronunciation
　Weak forms, linking and elision

see practice page 79

Lesson 2 *So far from home, so long ago*

Language focus:	Present perfect for recent events Clauses with past participles Collocations
Skills focus:	Listening to an extract from a novel read aloud for main idea and detail Speaking: talking about past events and changes in the present

1

Read the back cover of the novel below.

a What does it tell us about Eugenianus?
b The first part of the story is about Eugenianus' restoration to consciousness in a hospital in Northern Europe. What do you think might be the focus of the later part of the story?
c Which aspects of the book would you find most interesting?

EIGHT METRES DOWN IN THE ARCTIC ICE, AN OIL DRILL STRIKES INTO HUMAN FLESH. EIGHT METRES DOWN IS THE ICEBOUND BODY OF A MAN NINETEEN CENTURIES OLD …

A sentence of death – issued by a long-dead Roman emperor – has been halted by an accident of biology.

A brilliant Russian doctor and modern medical technology slowly restore the body to life …

THE MAN BROUGHT FROM HIS FROZEN TOMB IS LUCIUS AURELIUS EUGENIANUS, THE GREATEST OF ALL CAESAR'S GLADIATORS.

HIS STORY IS A SPELLBINDING CONFRONTATION OF ANCIENT WARRIOR AND MODERN WORLD … THE READER IS SWEPT TOWARDS ITS ULTIMATE CLIMAX IN ROME'S ETERNAL CITY …

FICTION
0 58 345097 0

ISBN 0-58-345097-0

9 780583 450973

U.K.   £1.25
Not for sale on Canada

2

The Roman gladiator, Eugenianus, has been revived but does not yet know that he has been 'dead' for nineteen centuries. He is being kept in a private ward lit by candles and Olava, one of his carers, speaks to him in Latin. He believes he has been captured by 'barbarians'. Now, suddenly frightened by something, he runs out of his room.

What things might Eugenianus see when he leaves his hospital room which would not have existed nineteen centuries ago, and which would alarm or confuse him?

3

 Listen to find out:

a the route Eugenianus follows when he leaves his room.
b where he goes to.

4

 As he runs through the hospital Eugenianus sees many unfamiliar things. Listen again and order the list of the things he sees.

a 'a small cubicle' ☐
b 'non-white vestments' ☐
c 'giant fat spear' ☐
d 'a sign in Roman language' ☐
e 'the entire ceiling aflame' ☐
f 'the metal door with no hands or pulleys' ☐
g 'the coarse white toga' ☐
h 'bright flames' ☐
i 'portal' ☐
j 'incense' ☐

Now work in pairs and decide what each expression refers to.
For example: 'a small cubicle' – the lift

5

How would Eugenianus have felt if he had run into your classroom? What would have been strange to him and how might he have described these things?

6

Choose another place you know well (eg a park, a cafe, a supermarket, your bedroom). Imagine you are Eugenianus. Write a paragraph describing what you see. Show your paragraph to the other people in the class and see if they can guess the place you have chosen and the things being described.

7

Imagine yourself in 30 years' time. Think about the following areas and note down your ideas.
– your family
– your job
– your achievements
– your English
– one bad thing that has happened to you
– one good thing that has happened to you
– your future plans

8

Imagine you are at a reunion of your English class in 30 years' time. Exchange information with the other people in the class to find out how your lives have changed and what you are doing now. Try to speak to at least five people.

9

Work in a group with some of the people you talked to. Make a poster giving some information about your group in 30 years' time.

Homework

Write a letter to someone in the class who missed the 30-year reunion telling them who you met there and what you found out about them.

Language Summary

Present perfect for recent events
  Eugenianus **has been revived** …

Clauses with past participles
  The man **brought from his frozen tomb** is Lucius Aurelius Eugenianus.

Collocations
  the **Arctic ice**

see practice page 80

Lesson 3 *How do you say it?*

Language focus:	Pronunciation and spelling British and American pronunciation
Skills focus:	Speaking: pronouncing difficult words

1

Work in pairs. These words are in phonemic script. What are they?

Now complete the poem with the words written in normal script.

Students of Accelerate

Advanced you are, but hesitate

Before you think you know the lot -

Our sounds can get you in a knot.

(1) _____ does not sound like ballet;

Comet, vomit, fillet, chalet;

Note the difference, moreover,

Between (2) _____ , lover, Dover.

(3) _____ , suite, ruin; walk and work,

Strangely, rhyme with hawk and shirk.

(4) _____ , but foul, and taunt, but aunt;

Font, front, (5) _____ ; want, grand, and grant,

Shoes, goes, does. Now first say: finger

And then: singer, (6) _____ , linger.

Sally, (7) _____ ; see and sea,

Eye, (8) _____ , aye and ski, key, quay!

Finally: which rhymes with 'tough',

Though, through, (9) _____ , cough, or enough?

Psychic, physics; (10)_____ , bomb, comb;

If I were you I'd stay at home!

/ˈwɒlɪt /
/ˈwəʊnt /
/ aɪ /
/ˈtuːm /
/ˈsəʊl /
/ˈdʒɪndʒə /
/ˈplaʊ /
/ˈælaɪ /
/ˈmuːvə /
/ˈsuːt /

2

Try reading the poem aloud with a partner.
 Then listen to the cassette to check
your pronunciation.

3

Work in groups. Think about these statements about
pronunciation. Do you agree with them? If not, how
would you reword them?

1 The sounds of English are more difficult to pronounce
than those of my language.
2 I think mistakes in word stress causes fewer problems
for the listener than mistakes in the pronunciation of
individual sounds.
3 I have problems in using weak forms appropriately.
For example: fish 'n' chips not fish and chips
4 I think intonation is probably picked up rather
than learnt.
5 My aim is to sound like a native speaker.

4

You will hear people from the places listed
below. Listen and identify the accents.

> *It's the way you talk*
> *that tells people about you, not*
> *what you say, isn't it?*
> *As soon as you open your mouth*
> *people can tell where you*
> *come from.*

Australia	☐	England	☐
Ireland	☐	Jamaica	☐
New York	☐	Scotland	☐
South Africa	☐	Wales	☐

Homework

Practise reading through the poem in Activity 1
until you can do it quickly and without hesitating.
See if you can think of some more examples and
add two more lines to the poem (you can add
them at any point).

5

Which of the accents do you find easiest to understand?
Which do you like most?
– Do you find any of the accents unattractive?
– Give examples of pronunciation features that helped
you identify the accents.
– How much does the pronunciation of your own
language vary?

6

Can you think of any ways in which British and
American pronunciation vary? Discuss with a
partner and give examples of words that are
pronounced differently.

7

Now listen to an extract from a lecture on
British and American pronunciation. Does the
lecturer mention any of the variations you thought of
in Activity 6?

8

Look at the examples below. Listen to the
lecture again and note down what features of
British and American pronunciation they demonstrate.

1 _____
eg medicine, secretary
2 _____
eg anti-aircraft, research, translate
3 _____
eg cigarette, laboratory, princess
4 _____
eg aunt, banana
5 _____
eg got, stop, lost
6 _____
eg duty, tune, new
7 _____
eg car, father
8 _____
eg Betty, writer

Now practise saying the words above with both
American and British accents.

Language Summary

Pronunciation and spelling
Our sounds can get you in a **knot**.

British and American pronunciation

see practice page 81

35

Lesson 1 *Singing solo*

Language focus:	*All, no; both, either, neither; each, every* Describing character Adverbs and adjectives with the same form
Skills focus:	Speaking: comparing impressions made by a newspaper and a song

1

Work in groups. Think of a famous singer or musician. What sort of person are they? Tick any words from the box below that describe them.

moody	☐	rebellious	☐	unspoiled	☐
weird	☐	mixed up	☐	shy	☐
extravagant	☐	natural	☐	brash	☐
reckless	☐	immature	☐	modest	☐
hard	☐	macho	☐	aggressive	☐
diffident	☐	highly-strung	☐	unaffected	☐
full of himself/herself	☐			flamboyant	☐

2

Look at the photo of the singer Joan Armatrading. What sort of person do you think she is?

3

Read the first part of the newspaper article about Joan Armatrading. What point is the first paragraph making about her character? How is this reinforced in the second paragraph?

The softer side of Joan Armour-plating

by Corinna Honan

When Joan Armatrading was being interviewed recently, she was asked how she'd cope with total isolation on a desert island. 'When can I go?' she said. Human company, it seems, holds no great attraction. Some weeks she never sees a person at all. Other people may find that strange, she says, but that's just how she is. Doesn't like people much, never did.

The first time I saw Joan on stage she was the support act to a flamboyant seventies super-group. Few in the audience had ever heard of her. She stood frozen at the microphone, a sturdy figure in jeans and T-shirt who might have strayed off a Birmingham market stall. But that extraordinary deep, swooping voice was enough to stop many mid-step in their drift to the bar …

(The Daily Mail)

4

Work in pairs. Here is the script of a Joan Armatrading song, to which extra words have been added. Before you listen, try to identify the extra words and put brackets round them.

Me Myself I

I sit here (all) by myself
And you know I (really) love it
You know that I don't
want someone
To come pay me a visit
I just wanna be by myself
I came in this world all alone
Me myself I

I want to go off to China
And to see Japan too.
I'd like to sail across the
oceans
before the seven seas run dry
I wanna go there by myself
I've just got room enough
for one
Me myself I

I wanna be a big shot
And have ninety fast cars
I wanna have a rich boyfriend
And a girl for laughs.
But only on a Saturday
Six days left to be alone
Me myself and I
Just me myself I

I don't want to be the bad guy.
Don't want to make a soul
start to cry
It's not that I only love myself
I just don't want
any company
Except for
Me myself I
Me myself … and I
Just me myself I.

5

Listen to the song and compare your script. How far does the song support the general image of Joan suggested by the text in Activity 3?

6

Think of six more adjectives beginning with 'self-' to add to this list.

1 self-absorbed
2 self-contained

7

Read the rest of the newspaper article about Joan Armatrading.

1 How many of the words you wrote in Activity 6 apply to Joan Armatrading?
2 List the similarities and the differences in the impression given of Joan in the song and in the newspaper article.

8

Work with a partner. Student A is Joan Armatrading, Student B is the interviewer, Corinna Honan. Roleplay the interview between them that was the basis for the newspaper article. Refer back to the song and article if necessary and add further questions and ideas of your own.

9

How much do you know about the background and personality of your favourite singer? Do they share any characteristics with Joan Armatrading?

Fortunately, her debilitating shyness has always been tempered with a rare sense of self-possession. It was already in place at seven when she left the West Indies to fly across the Atlantic alone to join her parents in Birmingham where her father was working for British Rail.

She still remembers her first experience of snow with wonderment, and how she insisted on running about barefoot at school, as she'd always done in the West Indies. But the Birmingham playground must have been a frighteningly alien place.

'I was painfully shy, and didn't have any special good friends at school,' she says. 'But it never really bothered me. I was very happy just being in the playground and watching everyone else play. I never wanted to be part of a gang. I just never liked people.

'I'd see how the children were with one another, all the bullying and each one trying to come out on top. It took me a long, long time to get to like people a bit. But I'm not totally convinced. I've always been on the outside, watching. That's why my songs are observation songs.'

Her isolation increased when she started secondary school and her mother fell ill. As the eldest girl of six children, it fell to Joan to skip large chunks of schooling and stay at home 'being a mother and cooking and ironing and all that stuff'. When she did get out, she'd go to movies and parks on her own. It was, she insists repeatedly, a very *happy* childhood.

Did she love her parents, you wonder? 'My mother is brilliant, a strong, good, kind, very intuitive woman. I can't tell you a lot about my father. I never took much notice of him.'

Now in her forties, she has no desire to marry. She loves the countryside, loves the lack of noise, the neighbours who keep a proper English distance. None of her hobbies involves human companionship. She goes fly-fishing. She enjoys ten-mile hikes, always alone. She likes making comic characters out of modelling clay.

Like many people with a talent for observation, she can be very good company. She may not like people much, but their emotional vagaries have always inspired songs that seem to come from the heart. To her, human nature holds endless fascination, providing it remains at a comfortable distance. Self-analysis does not interest her. 'I don't think I'm the only loner in the world. I can't explain why I am the way I am. I've always been a bit weird; can't help you really,' she says gently.

(The Daily Mail)

Homework

Write a poem about yourself called 'Me Myself I' using the Joan Armatrading song as a model.

Language Summary

All, no; both, either, neither; all, each, every
    ... ironing and **all** that stuff ...

Describing character
    I was **painfully shy**.

Adverbs and adjectives with the same form
    I came in this world all **alone**.

see practice page 82

Lesson 2 *Non-stop news*

Language focus:	Quantifiers
	Media vocabulary
	Talking about specific quantities
Skills focus	Reading an article for detail
	Writing: preparing a news broadcast

1

Find a word beginning with *news* for each of
the following:

1 **news** _____ : in Britain, a shop where newspapers and
magazines, as well as sweets, cigarettes and stationery,
are sold.

2 **news** _____ : an organisation that gathers news stories
from a particular country or from all over the world and
supplies them to journalists.

3 **news** _____ : an important item of news that TV or radio
companies broadcast as soon as they receive it, often
interrupting other programmes to do so.

4 **news** _____ : one or more printed sheets of paper
containing information about an organisation that is sent
regularly to its members.

5 **news** _____ : the British term for the American word
'newscaster'.

6 **news** _____ : a reporter on current affairs for
newspapers, radio or TV.

2

Discuss in pairs. What changes in technology might
have affected the role of a TV news correspondent
over the last ten or fifteen years?

3

You are going to hear a British news
correspondent talking about her work.

1 What is the main change she has seen in news
broadcasting?

2 What are the problems resulting from this change?

4

In the text she discusses some of the problems she
faced during one afternoon in her work as a war
correspondent. Read the text and underline the
main locations she visited.

One one occasion when I
was sent to cover a major
international crisis, I was
in the hotel bedroom that
was our headquarters. We
had three crews out at the
time, and two back at the
hotel. I then heard on the
two-way radio, at seven
minutes past 12, one of
our crews ferrying a
message: 'Firing has
begun. There is gunfire. There is gunfire in the area of
a hospital.' He named it. I knew the hospital. I could
hear the sound of heavy firing over the two-way radio.

I went with a crew, virtually hijacking a car. Within
seven minutes we were near that hospital, but there
was so much gunfire between us and the hospital I
never got there. In front of us was a horrendous scene,
one of great confusion that I did not fully understand
until days later. In fact, what was happening was that
the vehicles of the rebels, which had come in 24 hours
earlier, were sitting, abandoned, at a large street
intersection. They had been set on fire by some local
people and were now being crashed into by the
national army coming into town. None of that
information was available when I saw what was going
on; it was just a scene of confusion, a great deal of
shooting, quite a number of corpses, people being
shot in front of us. There was panic and a lot of people
running around on the outskirts, unaware of the
seriousness of the situation.

Question: Do you go back to the hotel and send off
what information you've got, or do you stay to find out
a bit more? When is your deadline? Is there someone
else from another news company going back to be the
first with the news? It is getting to be a more difficult
decision, especially as there are claims made now in
the competitive news media, particularly in the newer
ones, that being first at breaking the news is a great
prize we should win.

We stayed 45 minutes in that area, until it became
too difficult for us to remain. I then decided that I had to
get some idea of the damage being done; so I tried to
get to another hospital. Then we came across a group
of people with a woman very severely injured. We took
her in the car – one of the few vehicles on the road
that night – to hospital, and there I got some idea of
the scale of things, seeing something like 120 people
come past me, severely injured, with some dead. At
which point, again you think, do I get across town to go
on air? Or do I film more? Do I pull the crew out of
this? Do I want to be first, or do I want to be fullest?

(The Listener)

5

Look at the text again and decide whether the following statements are true (T) or false (F), or whether there is no evidence in the text (NE).

1 The crew who contacted her were near a hospital. ☐

2 She and another crew insisted on using someone else's car to get to the hospital. ☐

3 Local people were firing on the national army near the hospital. ☐

4 The crew were unaware of the seriousness of the situation. ☐

5 Her main priority was to be first with the news. ☐

6 The main reason for going to the second hospital was to help the injured woman. ☐

7 At the second hospital she realised that the conflict was more serious than they had earlier thought. ☐

8 She was afraid it was too dangerous for the crew to return across town to the hotel. ☐

6

Listen to the news broadcast covering the events described in the text on page 38. This is a 'first' broadcast – it gives only the information that the crew found out when they visited the area of fighting. What facts are **not** included in the broadcast?

7

Work in groups. Prepare a second news bulletin – a 'fullest' rather than a 'first' version – covering the same incident and using information from the text. Write out your bulletin. Your bulletin can include some of these phrases:

… information is beginning to come through …
… the latest stage in the conflict was sparked …
… it appears that …
… caught in the crossfire …
… we understand that …

8

Work in pairs. Make up three newspaper headlines for real or imaginary events in the place where you live. Write all three on a piece of paper. Pass your headlines on to another pair. Look at the new headlines you have received, choose one and plan a possible news report describing the event. Decide if you are preparing a 'first' or 'fullest' account.

Homework

Write up the news bulletin you prepared in Activity 7 in the form of a short script for a TV broadcast. Give brief details of any film footage that should be included.

Language Summary

Quantifiers
   … **none of** that information …

Media vocabulary

Talking about specific quantities
   an **item** of news

see practice page 83

Lesson 3 *On the box*

Language focus:	Omissions in colloquial English Noun modifiers
Skills focus:	Speaking: discussing technology Reading: to check predictions

1

Which of the things in the list below have you seen or used? Number them 1 to 8 according to how familiar you are with them (1 = most familiar).

a laptop	☐	**cable and satellite TV**	☐
CD ROM	☐	**computer games**	☐
e-mail	☐	**an electronic dictionary**	☐
the Internet	☐	**a video phone**	☐

Discuss your ranking with other students and find out about any items you are less familiar with.

2

Greg is a businessman who has to travel a lot. He has a young family. He is staying in a hotel in a city he has never visited before, and where he knows no one. The following day he has to make an important presentation. Here are some of the things he may want to do while in the hotel.

a buy tickets for music or sports events

b do some exercise in his room

c find out what's on in local cinemas and theatres

d have copies of letters read out aloud to him

e get an emergency dental appointment

f receive messages that have been sent to him at his office since he left

g rehearse his presentation and watch a recorded play-back

h see how his family are and say goodnight to his children

i send copies of important papers to his office

j send his wife a bunch of flowers

k watch a sports game and make bets on the action

Add two more items to the list, then discuss how present or future technology could help him do these things without leaving his hotel room.

3

Read the article on page 41 and find how many of the activities in Activity 2 are mentioned. Write the letter of each one referred to in the margin of the text. One has been done for you as an example.

Big Roles for the Little Screen

When you check in to the hotel room of the near future, the hotel TV won't be just for watching news programs.

Instead, the TV will be your on-the-road
5 command centre, offering far more than one-way entertainment. Plug in your laptop and
[f] create a giant monitor for reading e-mail and computer graphics. Eyes tired? Switch the TV to voice and it will read messages to you,
10 even those typed ones sent by e-mail.

The TV will tape your rehearsal of a business presentation and play it back. As a frequent business traveler, you often don't have the option of swinging by the store on
15 the way home from work. Order almost anything by using the TV. Forget to pack underwear? Order by 9 p.m. and overnight mail will arrive with a new pair by 6 a.m.

By using the remote control or touching
20 the screen you can buy tickets to a concert or baseball game. Restaurant reservations can also be made by a click of the remote control. Call up a list of nearby Italian restaurants, then look at a video of the interiors. Click on
25 the menu and view pictures of any dish. You'll even be able to smell the food, says Daniel Burrus, co-author of Technotrends.

It's bedtime for the children back home. Call them on the videophone and wish
30 them good night.

Bored? Watch almost any movie at any time, or the episode of the soap you missed two nights ago. Play Nintendo. Call up an exercise tape.

35 Or, watch a National Football League game. Score points each time you predict, say, if the next play will be a pass to the right or a run to the left. Play against others who are watching the game in their rooms.
40 Hotels will even make it interesting by awarding winners a free bottle of wine.

If you wake up in the middle of the night with chest pains, use the TV remote to call a doctor. The doctor will be able to access your
45 medical records from your regular doctor's computer. Sensors can transmit vital signs such as blood pressure, so the doctor can tell you whether it's merely heartburn.

'From the hotel TV you'll have total access
50 to information anywhere,' Burrus says. And you'll still be able to watch the news programs.

(USA Today)

4

In the text, underline the facilities that were *not* in the list in Activity 2.

5

Which three of the facilities described in the text or in the list would you like to have a) in a hotel room and b) at home? Compare your choice with a partner.

6

Find and underline these words in the text. Are they used as verbs or nouns?

> **plug   e-mail   switch   tape**
> **click   view   access**

7

 Listen to the extracts. Which of the TV services is Greg using in each case?

Homework

Write an information sheet describing the channels you have chosen giving a brief description of the types of programmes and details of any forthcoming special attractions for each channel.

8

Work in groups. Your institution is getting a cable TV system. You have been asked to choose eight channels for your class. Which ones would you choose to reflect the needs and interests of your class? Use the list below or think of your own ideas.

a 24-hour news channel	an English-language channel
a movie channel	a sports channel
a shopping channel	a quiz games channel
a business channel	a travel channel
a cartoon channel	a scientific/educational channel
a children's channel	a pop video channel
a country and western music channel	an arts channel (classical music, ballet, opera, etc)
a science fiction channel	a soap opera channel

9

Describe your channel selection to other groups, giving reasons for your choices.

Language Summary

Omissions in colloquial English
> **Eyes tired? Switch** the TV to voice **and** it will read messages to you.

Noun modifiers
> a **movie** channel

see practice page 84

Lesson 1 *Future shocks*

> **Language focus:** Future in the past
> Prefixes and suffixes
>
> **Skills focus:** Listening to and reading accounts
> of the same event

1

Classify these words as positive, negative or neutral.

> anticipation   expectation   far-sighted
> foreboding   forecast   forewarn
> forward planning   omen   ominous
> prediction   premonition   promising
> prophecy   sinister   vision

2

Listen to Susan King talking about a frightening experience.

1 Who do you think she is speaking to? When and where might she be speaking?

2 Which of the following information does she include?

– the date of the incident
– the type of plane
– the nationality of most of the people in it
– where she was sitting
– why she was travelling
– what caused the accident
– the number of survivors
– the time she woke up

3 How did Susan feel after the dream? Have you ever had a dream that frightened you?

3

Listen again to an extract from the same recording. Add words to make an exact transcript of what Susan says.

and

,awful shaking

‸suddenly the plane started shaking‸from side to side, and then it plunged down. Then I don't know what happened but I know everything was quiet and there were pine trees. It was horrible.

4

Now read the extract from a magazine article about Susan's experience. What are the main differences between the spoken and written accounts?

Susan King woke up shivering. It was a while before she realised she was safely at home in bed. Only minutes before she had been thousands of miles away. In her dream, Susan had been sitting in row 52 of a plane, and could see dark heads in front of her, talking a foreign language. 'I was two people,' she says, 'one who had to make this journey and one who was safe, far away.' Suddenly the plane started shaking from side to side and plunged downwards – and then there was silence. Susan was aware of the pungent aroma of pine trees and the sickening stillness of death all around her. And then she woke up. It was 3.35 in the morning …

(Options)

Now discuss the following points with a partner and write notes.

– the way the information is organised
– sentence length and the way the sentences are constructed and linked
– repetition
– use of direct speech
– vocabulary (what sort of words are added in the written passage?)

5

Listen to a TV news extract from August 2 1985, less than three weeks after Susan's dream. Make notes about the information given.

6

Compare your notes with a partner and together write a second paragraph for the magazine article describing how Susan's dream came true. Include information about Susan's reaction to the news. Begin like this:

Less than three weeks later, …

7

Read the following account of a different incident. Find
four similarities and four differences in the two incidents.

One Saturday morning Chris Robinson woke up suddenly
and reached for the notepad beside his bed. His dream had
been particularly vivid – a mid-air explosion of two Russian
planes that looked like fireworks, and the pilots bailing out in
parachutes. Chris, a radio and TV engineer, knew that a real-
life disaster was about to happen. A few hours later he saw
an ad for an international air display which was to include
aeronautical acrobatics. He drove there to try to avert a
crash he now knew was going to happen. At the entrance
he told the policeman, 'Look, you may not believe this, but
two planes are going to crash when they come down from
the loop-the-loop.' The policeman just waved him on. Ten
minutes later two Soviet MiG planes exploded in a shower
of fireworks. And, sure enough, two parachutes then
detached themselves from the smoke and drifted safely
downwards. Chris recalls, 'I felt a mixture of shock and
excitement at what I'd seen – it was identical to my dream.'

8

Work in groups. Make up a story about a dream that
came true. Your dream can be a good or a bad one,
but it should *not* be about an accident. Use two of
these images:
– a tree with fragrant white flowers
– a book with missing pages
– a stone face on a mountain
– a dog with one blue eye and one brown
– an empty garden with children's voices
– water trickling down a path

9

When your story is ready, find a partner from another
group and tell one another your stories.

Homework

Write your story from Activities 8 and 9 in the
form of a magazine article, changing the wording
and organisation where necessary to make the
style suitable for a written account.

Language Summary

Future in the past
   A real life disaster **was about to** happen …

Prefixes and suffixes

see practice page 85

Lesson 2 *Fatal mistake?*

Language focus: Reporting verbs
Medical vocabulary
Expressions describing state of health
Voluntary and involuntary activities

Skills focus: Reading and reacting to a
newspaper article
Speaking: roleplay

1

Put the words below in order to make a newspaper headline.

DEAD PRONOUNCED SAYS 'I WAS
'FINE' AM FEELING WOMAN
WHO

2

The headline comes from a news story. Work with a partner and write five questions that you would expect to be answered in the article. Compare with another pair and add to your list.

3

Read the newspaper article below and look for the answers to your questions.

The woman who came back from the dead said yesterday that she felt fine as the doctor who declared her dead apologised. Dorothy Turner, who is still recovering in hospital, looked pale but was able to walk unaided as she appeared with her husband, Stan, at a news conference. She refused to comment on her experience and would only say, 'I'm fine, thank you.'

Her solicitor, William Evans, said that Mrs Turner, 61, had attempted suicide with an overdose of tablets at her home on New Year's Eve. Michael Lloyd, her doctor, wrongly declared her dead.

Mr Evans said: 'Dorothy and Stan Turner have had the opportunity of reflecting carefully over the recent traumatic events and the various options open to them. They have decided not to make any formal complaint to the Family Health Services Authority or the General Medical Council. They have also decided that they do not wish to institute legal proceedings. Obviously the doctor in question made an error of judgement, but luckily the error has not had fatal consequences.'

He added: 'The family are just extremely grateful and relieved that Dorothy is alive and making very good progress. Dorothy unfortunately suffers from epilepsy. As a result, she was not able to drive. Because of her increasing years, she was no longer able to walk into the village, some distance from her home.

She felt very lonely and isolated and started to suffer from depression.

'On New Year's Eve it came to a head. She could not face going on. She took a large quantity of her epilepsy tablets and also some sleeping tablets. She climbed into bed and just drifted off to sleep.'

Mr Evans said Mr Turner had found his wife in the early hours of New Year's Day. He had called the ambulance service who arranged for a GP to attend the home. Dr Lloyd examined Mrs Turner and told Mr Turner she was dead. The doctor then called an undertaker.

John Thompson, the undertaker and a family friend, spotted a vein twitching, then heard her snore, soon after she was delivered to the hospital mortuary at about 4.30 am. An emergency resuscitation team was called and she was taken to an intensive care ward. After three days in intensive care Mrs Turner was transferred to a general ward. Mr Evans said that Mrs Turner and her husband wished to thank all hospital staff, wellwishers, and the undertakers for their 'timely alertness'.

(The Times)

4

In the text, find:

1 six words referring to jobs/work

_____

_____

2 four expressions relating to medicine and treatment

_____

_____

3 three legal expressions

_____

_____

4 the names of three places in a hospital

_____

_____

5

Discuss how you think Mrs Turner and her husband were feeling a) before this happened and b) after Mrs Turner's recovery.

6

Choose one of the following people and think of some questions you would like to ask them.

The woman
The solicitor
The husband
The family friend
The doctor

_____

_____

_____

7

Find a partner and ask them to roleplay the person you have chosen and to answer the questions you prepared in Activity 6. Then take on the role of the person your partner wants to interview and answer their questions.

Homework

Write the statement that the doctor gave the police after the incident, including some or all of the expressions below.

Mrs Turner has been my patient for …
She had been suffering from …
I was called to the house at approximately …
I found the patient lying …
On examination, I …
The cause of death appeared to be …
Following this, …

Language Summary

Reporting verbs
    … a woman who was **pronounced** dead …

Medical vocabulary
    An emergency **resuscitation** team was called.

Expressions describing state of health
    … said that she felt **fine**.

Voluntary and involuntary activities
    … saw a vein **twitch**

see practice page 86

45

Lesson 3 *The journal of a ghosthunter*

Language focus: Expressing general beliefs
Vocabulary of fear and of enthusiasm

Skills focus: Speaking: problem solving
Reading for detail

1

Most cultures have legends of ghosts – but ghosts from different places behave in different ways. In this puzzle you have to share information to find out about five ghosts which appeared in different parts of the world. Work in groups of 4–6. You will hear twelve sentences describing five ghosts.

Each of you should try to make notes of the information in two or three of the sentences. Before you begin, decide together which sentences each member of the group will make notes on.
After listening, combine your information to sort out descriptions of the five ghosts and complete the table below.

Ghost's nationality	Physical description	Activity	Place seen
German			

2

Look at the photos below. They come from a book by Simon Marsden. What do you think the book is about?

3

You are going to hear an interview with Simon Marsden. This was later used as the basis for a short magazine article. Before you listen, read the outline of the article below. Then listen and make notes of the relevant information. Finally, use your notes to complete the article below.

Simon Marsden is a self-confessed ghost freak. His latest book '_____' contains _____ . As a child, _____ _____ His career started when _____ . He believes that _____ _____ 'People say I'm a masochist,' he says, 'But _____ '

4

Read Simon Marsden's account of his visit to Dracula's palace.

1 The passage contains ten words referring to the terrible activities of the tyrant. Underline the words and check the meanings of any unknown ones with a dictionary.

2 The following phrases were removed from the text. Try to replace them correctly.

1 During his lifetime
2 to beg forgiveness from God for his crimes
3 where I came across two gravestones
4 who ruled this corner of Romania through a reign of terror
5 women and children

It's easy to forget that Dracula was a real person in the fifteenth century. Tirgoviste was his capital city and the palace proved to be an ideal platform for the tyrant to enjoy the many impalements and tortures carried out in the courtyard below. He is said to have blinded, strangled, hanged, burned, skinned, roasted, hacked and buried alive over 100,000 men. Very little remains of the actual state buildings except the crumbling walls above the dark vaults where Dracula would often retreat. When I had seen enough, I walked into a nearby field. I resolved to carry some garlic with me during the rest of my travels in Romania.

(Options)

5

Work in groups. Think of a place in your country which has a story or legend associated with it and tell other people in your group about it. If you have actually visited the place, tell the group your impressions.

Homework

Either write a letter to Simon Marsden telling him about the place you described in Activity 7, explaining why he could add it to his next book, and suggesting what sort of photograph he could take.
Or write an explanation to accompany one of the photos from Simon's book in Activity 2.

Language Summary

Expressing general beliefs
    '**People say** I'm a masochist.'

Vocabulary of fear
    ... **haunts** the **dark graveyard** ...

Vocabulary of enthusiasm
    a self-confessed ghost **freak**

see practice page 87

Lesson 1 *Chindogu – alternative products*

Language focus:	Infinitives and split infinitives
	Infintive and *-ing* complements after nouns
Skills focus:	Reading and writing a humorous description of a new product

1

Look at this picture. What do you think this product is for?
Now read the text and answer the questions below.

Walk 'n' Wash
Makes washing days a stroll in the park

Some choices are hard, especially when guilt enters the picture. You'd like to go for a walk, but you ought to be doing the laundry. Well, now you can do both. The Walk 'n' Wash comprises a pair of polythene tanks, one for each leg, with the capacity to hold two litres of laundry and water. So it's wash on the right leg, then rinse on the left (or vice versa, according to your personal preference). The weight of the tanks turns walking into a workout, making this a triple-barrelled Chindogu.

(Unuseless Japanese Inventions)

1 What do you think is the main purpose of the text? How serious is it?

2 Number these topics in order, to show how the text is organised.

   a how the product works ☐
   b why the product is needed ☐
   c an extra advantage of the product ☐
   d a slogan describing it ☐

3 The Walk 'n' Wash is described as 'triple-barrelled'. This suggests it has three uses. What are they?

4 How does the writer use the language of the text to involve the reader directly? Give some examples.

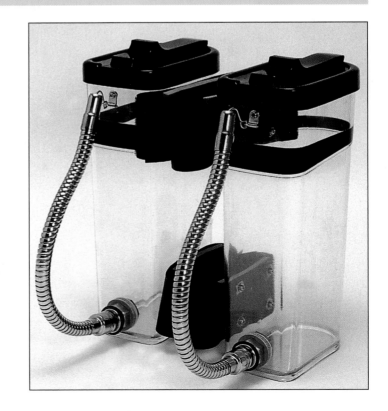

2

The Walk 'n' Wash is an example of a Chindogu – a type of invention which was originally developed (not too seriously!) in Japan. Look at the photos below of another Chindogu. Can you work out what it is for? Think of a name for it.

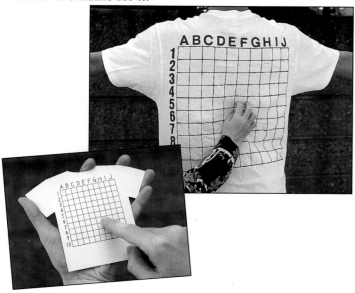

3

Work with a partner. Write a description of the Chindogu in Activity 2. Follow the structure and style of the description you identified in Activity 1 above. Remember to include a slogan as well.

4

Compare your description with the one on page 66. Did you think of the same use for the Chindogu? Did the style of your description involve the reader in the same way as the passage?

Homework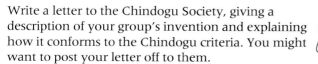

Write a letter to the Chindogu Society, giving a description of your group's invention and explaining how it conforms to the Chindogu criteria. You might want to post your letter off to them.

Chindogu Society Home Office
Flower Building, 5th Floor
1 – 25 – 3 Hongo
Bunkyo-ku, Tokyo 114, Japan

5

The creator, Kenji Kawakami, has described ten characteristics of a Chindogu. Look at the list of characteristics and discuss what you think they mean.

a A Chindogu cannot be for real use.
b You must be able to actually make a Chindogu.
c There is a little anarchy in the creation of every Chindogu.
d Chindogu are tools for everyday life.
e Chindogu are not for sale.
f Humour must not be the sole reason for creating a Chindogu.
g Chindogu are not made for propaganda.
h Chindogu are never taboo.
i Chindogu belong to everyone.
j Chindogu are without prejudice.

6

Listen to the explanations of the ten characteristics and match each one to one of the sentences in Activity 5.

7

Choose one of the Chindogu you have looked at in this lesson. How far does it conform to these characteristics?

8

Work in groups and invent a new Chindogu. You may use one of the ideas below, or make up your own. Remember! Your Chindogu must have the characteristics described in Activity 5.

– an invention to keep your shoes dry in the rain
– a way of keeping pens from rolling away which also acts as decoration
– a way to dry the washing while taking part in a sport
– a way of involving your pets in the housework
– a gadget for travellers

Describe your invention to the class, showing them an illustration if possible.

Language Summary

Infinitives and split infinitives
    They **must not be sold** even as a joke.
    You must be able **to actually make** a Chindogu.

Infinitive and *-ing* complements after nouns
    a way **to dry** the washing

see practice page 88

Lesson 2 *Everything but the kitchen sink*

Language focus: Complex sentences
Vocabulary of house and home
Pronunciation: homographs

Skills focus: Writing: recreating a complex sentence
Reading and summarising a text

1

As a class, discuss some of the things you did that your parents complained about when you were young.
Do you still do any of those things now?

2

Listen to three people talking about annoying habits.

1 Are any of the habits shown in the cartoon mentioned?
2 List the other habits mentioned.

3

The news item below consists of three sentences. Read the first and last sentences and then combine all the phrases given below to write one middle sentence. Do not change, add or delete any words.

The story of Paul Marriot and Tony Jeever must have sent a shiver down the spines of flatmates all over the country last week.

The two men,_____

_____

_____

_____

Jeever survived the attack and last week Marriot was sent to a secure psychiatric unit by a crown court judge.

clutching a carving knife,
had a row over the washing-up
Jeever woke up to find Marriot
shouting 'You are going to die!'
standing by the bedroom door
that one night two years later,

(1) The two men,
when they were living apart,
which grew into a dispute of such passion
which he then plunged into his former flatmate.
who shared a house in Cambridge,

Compare what you have written with another student.

Kitchen sink dramas

They hog the bathroom, steal your milk and never, ever wash up.
ROLAND WHITE on the horror of flatmates.

It always seems such a good idea at first, moving to the big city with your friends. 'Why don't we all live together? It'll be brill!'

It is only after the deposit has been paid and the posters taped to the walls that flatmates discover that life together might not be so brill after all, that Darren's socks are a stranger to washing powder, that Emma likes to clip her toenails while she watches television, and that Robert eats nothing but packet curry and individual fruit pies.

Before long, little notes begin to appear about the house. 'Would whoever is leaving toenail clippings in the TV lounge please clear them up!' and 'Don't

forget to clean the bath; it is not pleasant for the next person!' and 'Please do not ask to borrow my hair dryer as a refusal often offends.' By the time Darren, Emma and Robert have started to mark their milk with a felt-tipped pen, it is time to look for somewhere else to live, which means breaking up the bath-cleaning rota, the fridge-cleaning rota, the hedge-clipping rota and the dishwashing rota.

For those of a confrontational nature, flatmates offer endless possibilities. There are not only rows about washing up, but rows about noises, hot water, the vacuum cleaner, the telephone, the rent, cleaning the windows, playing the saxophone at 11.30 at night, going out

with each other's girlfriends, going out with each other's boyfriends and – worst of all – going out with each other.

Eventually, the flatmates drift away. They buy their own homes, they move away for work, or they get married. And it is always such fun, isn't it, for the young couple setting up on their own for the first time?

'Who forgot to clean the bath?'
'Well, it wasn't me.'
'Oh, no? And why do you always leave your socks on the floor, and why don't you clear away your nail clippings, and why can't you put the top back on the toothpaste, and I do wish you wouldn't keep on using my hair dryer …'

(The Sunday Times)

4

1 Complete each line with a maximum of eight words to summarise the main ideas of the article above.

At first, _____

However, soon _____

In the end _____

And then _____

2 List all the causes of friction between flatmates mentioned in the article.
Which of the habits would annoy you most? Discuss with a partner.

3 Is the main purpose of the article:
  a to entertain?
  b to warn?
  c to advise?

5

Discuss in groups.

1 What assumptions can you make from the above article about the way young people live in Britain? For example: Young people may live away from their families for some years.

2 Which aspects of the culture of flatsharing described in the article seem 'foreign' to you?

3 In your own culture, is it usual for young people to live away from home, and if so, what sort of problems do they face in adapting to a new life style? If not, what sort of problems may arise at home?

Homework

Think about a major change that took place in your life in the past – or a change that may be going to occur. Write a letter to yourself at that time – past or future – with advice on how to cope with that change.

Language Summary

Complex sentences
  The two men, who shared a house in Cambridge
  … his former flatmate.

Vocabulary of house and home
  … who shared **a house** in Cambridge …

Pronunciation: homographs
  … had **a row** over the washing up …

see practice page 89

Lesson 3 *Cyberstory*

Language focus:	Phrasal verbs Giving more information about adjectives Idioms with the word *hot*
Skills focus:	Speaking: discussing texts from different sources Reading and writing film reviews

1

What could these phrases all refer to?

2

 Listen to check your predictions.

3

 Listen to the next part of the talk and list nine ways in which this medium is different from conventional writing.

_____

_____

_____

_____

_____

_____

_____

_____

_____

4

Cyber – prefix – connected with computers, especially with the sending of messages on the Internet

Discuss the possible meaning of 'cyber-terrorist'.

5

Work with a partner. Student A reads the text on page 53 and Student B reads the text on page 66.

1 How are cyber-terrorists involved in the film plot?

2 Find which sections of your text are mainly about:

  a the setting of the film.
  b the plot.
  c the reviewer's evaluation.

3 List some examples from your text of:

  a words connected with computers
  b colloquial language
  c language related to films

4 Now compare the information from your text with your partner's. Are there any differences between the two reviews and the emphasis they give?

6

With your book closed, imagine you and your partner have both seen this film. Discuss together what you liked and disliked about it and whether you would recommend it to other people.

FILMS – THE NET (12)

FIVE STEPS TO SURVIVING THE NET

STEP ONE – WHAT IS THE NET?

The Net is an abbreviation for the Internet – a complex network of information that can be accessed by any computer, so long as you have the technological know-how. This means you get to sit in front of your computer all day and do clever things like order pepperoni pizza and chat to other faceless people with strange names like Cyberbob and Iceman!

STEP TWO – WHY IS THIS A PROBLEM?

Well, it's not unless you're Angela Bennett played by Sandra Bullock – computer wiz extraordinaire. Then you have a big problem because Cyberterrorists are after you. They have a plot to take over the world by logging into the Net and accessing top secret computers and you've stumbled across them.

STEP THREE – ARE THEY DANGEROUS?

Extremely, because they can literally delete your life without firing a single shot. In the case of Angela this means she wakes up one day to find all her computer records have been changed. Instead of being a harmless computer wiz from Dullsville, she is now a criminal called Ruth wanted by the police.

STEP FOUR – WHAT DO YOU DO NEXT?

Well, firstly you fall in love with one of the Cyberterrorists because you don't know he's out to kill you. Then you discover his dirty little game, so you run for your life. Next you try to prove you're not a criminal, but a harmless wiz. However, no one believes you, so you end up in jail, which leaves you with just one option – go back to what you know best and try and beat the baddies at their own game.

STEP FIVE – IS IT WORTH SEEING?

Does Arnold Schwarzenegger have muscles? If you want pure white-knuckle-clenching action, nail-biting intrigue and a chance to see Sandra Bullock at her best then see this today!

(Smash Hits)

Homework

Choose a film you have seen recently and write a review for a pop magazine following the format of one of the reviews. You should include information on the background and setting of the film, the plot and an evaluation of the film and the acting.

Language Summary

Phrasal verbs
You **end up** in jail.

Giving more information about adjectives
pretty weird

Idioms with the word *hot*
a **hot-shot** computer expert

see practice page 90

Lesson 1 *A sense of place*

Language focus:	Definite and indefinite articles
	Literary language
Skills focus:	Reading: reacting to written texts
	Writing a description of a place

a

1

Discuss these pictures. Do they remind you of any experiences in your own life? How many of your five senses – sight, hearing, taste, touch, smell – does each picture appeal to?

b

c

d

e

2

The extracts below and on page 55 are from books set in five different parts of the world. Read each extract and underline the links with the five pictures above.

1

By this time the sun was driving broad golden spokes through the lower branches of the mango-trees; the parakeets and doves were coming home in their hundreds; and shufflings and scufflings in the branches showed that the bats were ready to go out on the night-picket. Swiftly the light gathered itself together, painted for an instant the faces and the cart-wheels and the bullocks' horns as red as blood. Then the night fell, changing the touch of the air, drawing a low, even haze like a fine blue veil, across the face of the country and bringing out, keen and distinct, the smell of wood-smoke and cattle and the good scent of wheaten cakes cooked on ashes.

(Kim)

2

The temperature drops thirty degrees in four hours, and the sea grows as motionless as a mirror. The clouds and the sea now glide together in a curtain of heavy grey silk. The water grows viscous and tinged with pink, like a liqueur of wild berries. A blue fog of frost smoke detaches itself from the surface of the water and drifts across the mirror. Then the water solidifies. Out of the dark sea the cold now pulls up a rose garden, a white blanket of ice blossoms formed from salt and frozen drops of water.

(Miss Smilla's Feeling for Snow)

3

Notes for landscape tones. Long sequences of tempera. Light filtered through the essence of lemons. An air full of brick dust – sweet smelling brick dust – and the odour of hot pavements slaked with water. Light damp clouds, earth-bound yet seldom bringing rain. Upon this squirt dust-red, dust-green, chalk-mauve and watered crimson.

(Justine)

4

The bush spreads in gentle folds to the horizon: dusty eucalyptus, tawny grass, grey fleeces, smoke-blue wattle … Looking across the endless spread of gum trees and banksias, shimmering blue in a eucalyptus haze and the cliffs dropping into fern-filled canyons … no evidence of man's presence mars the ancient terracotta cliffs: not a single tree or shrub was planted by human hand; the land itself, a national park, was not owned by any one person. All this is thrilling, after the cultivated landscapes of Europe where generations have trod, have trod…

(The Observer)

5

There is a tiny bay half-shut in by rocks, and smothered by olive woods that slope down swiftly. Then there is one pink, flat fisherman's house. You run out of the gate into the sea, which washes among the rocks at the mouth of the bay… softly and nicely, with just a bit of white against the rocks. Figs and grapes are ripe. Think, we can sit round the open chimney at night, and burn olive wood, and hear the sea washing.

(A Book of Traveller's Tales)

3

The five texts are about five of the regions in the box. Read the texts again and suggest which region each is describing. Which parts of the texts helped you to decide?

| **Africa** **Europe** **North America** **Australia** |
| **The Far East** **India** **South America** **the Arctic** |

4

Look at the texts again and discuss these questions with a partner. Which text or texts:
1 do you like best?
2 could have come from a novel?
3 could be part of a letter?
4 make the most effective use of colour?
5 could have been written by a painter?

5

From the five texts, choose one that you find appeals the most to your senses – sight, smell, taste, hearing, touch. Read it carefully then close your book and write down all the words connected with the senses that you can remember. Compare with another student who chose the same text. Which words or expressions did you both find most memorable?

Homework

Choose the most effective of the notes you wrote for Activity 7 as the basis for a paragraph creating a 'sense of place' of your own.

6

Listen. You are going to make a journey. When you have returned, tell your partner about the place you travelled to and what you experienced there.

7

With a partner decide on a place you both know well. Together, write phrases about:
– the exact colours of three things you see.
– two sounds.
– something living and the way it moves.
– something non-living and the way it feels.
– a smell or a taste.

Language Summary

Definite and indefinite articles
 the sea grows as motionless as **a** mirror

Literary language
 The sun was drawing broad golden spokes through the branches.

see practice page 91

Lesson 2 *First language, last language*

> **Language focus:** Position of adverbials
> Idioms to do with talking
> Collocations with the word *language*
> Overview of verb forms
>
> **Skills focus:** Speaking: talking about language,
> doing a survey

1

Work in groups. Try to think of one language beginning with each letter of the alphabet. The group with the most languages after five minutes is the winner.

Arabic , B ..., C ...

2

You are going to hear recordings of five of the languages below. Listen and see how many of the languages you can identify.

> **German   Chinese   English   Hindi   Arabic**
> **Navaho (a native American language)**
> **Russian   Spanish   Welsh   Zulu   Japanese**

Suggest some words to describe the sounds of each language.
For example: harsh, melodic, ...

3

The box above includes the five most widely-spoken languages in the world. Which do you think they are? Which of the languages in the box do you think has the *smallest* number of speakers?

4

Read the text below and think of five questions you would have liked to ask Red Thunder Cloud before he died.

Language dies with tribal elder

New York: A senior member of the Catawba tribe has died, taking with him the language of his people. Red Thunder Cloud, who was 76, will be buried in Massachusetts today. He used the language daily to say his prayers, although only his dog understood him in the end. 'The dog always seemed to know what he was saying,' said Lenora Penn, his closest friend. Thunder Cloud learnt Catawba on the knee of his grandfather, Strong Eagle. About 100 native American languages are still in use.

Compare your questions with other groups and choose the five most interesting questions.

5

Choose one person in the class to take the role of Red Thunder Cloud. Ask him your group's questions.

6

Work in groups. Imagine that your own language is under threat and is in danger of dying out. Discuss some of the reasons why your language should not be lost. For example:

– the historical links of the language with your country (including any legends about how it began)
– its use in literature
– the way it sounds
– its richness in terms of vocabulary, idioms, etc
– how it links you to other cultures and countries

Make a poster summarising some of the key points of your discussion and present it to the class.

Homework

Write the results of your survey from Activity 7 in the form of a short report.

7

You are going to do a survey about languages in your class. Choose one of the topics below for your survey.

1 How confident would you feel using a) your own language and b) English in each of the following situations:

– talking to a doctor
– giving a statement to the police
– comforting a very young child
– dealing with a long recorded telephone message
– leaving a message on an answerphone
– having an argument with a stranger
– making a speech at a public function
– bargaining in a market

Add three more situations of your own.

2 How many languages do you know? How well do you speak and write each one? What are your feelings about each of these languages and the cultures they are related to? What other languages would you like to learn and why?

3 Which language do you think:

a would be most difficult to learn?
b would be easiest to learn?
c sounds particularly attractive?
d is most useful?
e has the most interesting writing system?
f is the most romantic?

Add three more questions of your own.

Language Summary

Position of adverbials
Red Thunder Cloud, …, will be buried in Massachusetts **today**.

Idioms to do with talking

Collocations with the word *language*
widely-spoken languages

Overview of verb forms

see practice page 92

Lesson 3 *Fitting in*

Language focus:	Advice
	Fixed pair expressions
	Words from other languages
Skills focus:	Listening to advice on travelling
	Speaking: cultural differences

1

Divide the following words into two groups: those which go with 'travel' and those which go with 'culture'.

> **vulture   bug   agency   guide   gap**
> **brochure   sick   shock   iron   adapter**

Can you think of any more words related to 'travel' and 'culture'?

2

Listen and choose from the box and the photos the place you think each speaker could be talking about. Make notes of the things that helped you to decide.

> **California   Kenya   Turkey   Britain**
> **Saudi Arabia   Amsterdam   Indonesia**

3

 Now listen to some more clues to check which place each extract was about.

4

Now answer the following questions.

a Have you visited any of the places talked about? In your experience, is the advice given useful?

b What general topics were covered by the speakers?

c What other features can distinguish one country from another?

5

Your teacher will give you the name of a country on a label. Everyone except you will be able to see this label. You have to find out which is 'your' country by asking yes/no questions.

6

 Listen again to the first recording from Activity 2 and tick the expressions you hear.

a Take great care with … ☐
b It's probably best to … ☐
c It's usually better to … ☐
d It's easy to be caught out by … ☐
e … are the order of the day. ☐
f You'll also need … ☐
g … is a potential hazard ☐
h Take great care not to … ☐
i … can be a good idea. ☐
j There are no requirements for … ☐
k Remember that … ☐
l … is essential. ☐
m will stick out like a sore thumb … ☐
n You're expected to be … ☐
o … could offend some people … ☐
p … if possible, avoid … ☐

Homework

Write a paragraph for a guidebook aimed at younger English-speaking tourists giving advice on how to behave when visiting your country, and explaining some of the special features of your culture.

7

Work in groups. How important is your own culture to you, and how much do you know about it? Discuss some of these questions.

1 Do you know many traditional songs in your own language? When and where did you last sing or listen to a traditional song?

2 How many of your country's typical dishes can you prepare? Would you rather eat traditional food, or go to an American style restaurant?

3 Do you ever wear traditional dress or national costume?

4 Do you know any traditional national dances? When did you last do this sort of dancing?

5 When did you last go to see a film made in your own country?

6 What language does your favourite singer or group perform in?

7 Think of one aspect of 'imported' culture that you are happy to accept, and one that you are less happy about.

Language Summary

Advice
Take great care with …

Fixed pair expressions
hard and fast rules

Words from other languages

see practice page 93

Lesson 1 *The roots of happiness*

Language focus:	Verbs with fixed prepositions
	Colloquial ways of expressing emotions
Skills focus:	Listening for main idea
	Writing a haiku

1

Look at the table below. Choose four of the times given and in column A, note down exactly what you were doing at those times on one day in the last week. Then in column B, give each activity a 'Happiness rating' of between 1 and 10 (10 = the most happy, 1 = the least happy).

	A	B
7.30 am		
11.15 am		
2.25 pm		
5.05 pm		
8.45 pm		
11.15 pm		

Compare with another student. What were the high points of your days?

2

Discuss with the same person what could bring you happiness:

a over the next 24 hours.
b in the next week.
c in the next year.
d for the rest of your life.

Tell the class about some of the things that would make you and your partner happy. What are the most frequently mentioned things in each category above?

3

Look at the notice which was written by James Stone. What does it tell us about James Stone's present lifestyle and his beliefs? What else can you guess from the pictures?

Welcome friend. I hope you enjoy being in my cozy little home. I would like to introduce myself a little. I believe in equality and sharing. I live on about $100 a month. If you have less income than this and you need something that is here, please consider it a gift. There is food in the cupboard if you are hungry. Drinking water is in the bottle on the counter.
Peace and good wishes
James Stone
Message phone 311 7196

P.S. If you make your living by theft, don't bother to search for money because I don't have any here. If you are in a financial emergency, leave a note or a phone message for me. I can't promise anything but who knows, we might think of something together.

4

James Stone used to be an affluent college professor with a huge six-bedroom house in downtown Eugene, in Oregon, USA. List some possible differences between James' past and present lifestyles and suggest some reasons for the change.

5

 Listen to the first part of the interview and find out what his actual reason was.

6

 Listen to the next part of the interview and answer these questions.

1 How does James manage to survive on his present income?
2 What does he do about housing, food and other material goods?
3 What does he find the best thing about the change he has made in his lifestyle?
4 What features of his old lifestyle does he miss?
5 What happened to all his money?

7

What is your reaction to James' beliefs and actions? Would you ever consider doing something similar?

8

Work in pairs. Roleplay an interview with someone who has changed his or her lifestyle drastically. It could be for one of the following reasons:

a winning a lot of money
b marrying a famous person
c selling all their possessions to travel the world
d giving birth to quadruplets

Homework

Write a short newspaper article about the person in the interview in Activity 8.

Language Summary

Verbs with fixed prepositions
   I believe **in** equality …

Colloquial ways of expressing emotions
   I'm **happy as a clam**.

see practice page 94

Lesson 2 *What then?*

Language focus: Discourse in written text
Prepositions
Fixed phrases

Skills focus: Prediction and interpretation of spoken and written text

1

In groups, discuss some of the people who have been famous in your lifetime (eg sports players, entertainers, politicians). What were some of the factors that made them successful? Do you know where they are now and what they are doing?

2

Read the extract from a magazine article about an Olympic sports star, Steven Redgrave. What is the sport he is training for? Suggest some possibilities.

> Monday morning in the Leander club gym. Sixty minutes in the life of an Olympian.
> - Bench pull: 55kg weights, 50 repetitions (reps).
> - Sit-up on incline: 10 kilos, 20 reps.
> - Leg press: 20 reps.
> - Press-up: 20 reps.
> - Knives (throwing feet and arms upwards): 20 reps.
> - Rowing on a box, 10 kilos in each hand: 30 reps.
> - Angel (lie face down, lift arm and leg): 5 kilos, 20 reps.
> - Squat jump: 30 reps.
> - Lateral pull: 50 kilos, 20 reps.
> - Leg curl: 30 kilos, 20 reps.
> - Side bend: 45 kilos, 20 reps.
> - Step-up: 50 kilos, 20 reps. (10 on each leg)
> - Rowing machine; 20 quick strokes.
>
> This is one circuit. Medium weights – nothing too heavy – high repetition, high intensity. Heart and lungs under pressure, aerobic power in every breath, pushing muscles beyond the boundaries of endurance. Within the hour it is repeated four times. By the end of the session he is sweating profusely. His hair is matted to his head, his t-shirt streaked with damp. He winds down with swigs from a huge glass of diluted fruit juice.
>
> (The Sunday Times)

3

Cover up the magazine article in Activity 2.

1 Try to list all the words used for different parts of the body. Then look and check.
2 What words and phrases in the second paragraph tell us about the physical effort involved in the training programme?

4

Read the next extract, which is about Steve's memories of his last Olympic victory and then discuss the answers to the questions below in pairs.

Steve   Matt

> Sunday morning on Lake Piediluco, Italy. Seven minutes in the life of an Olympian ... Jurgen Grobler, the coach, called them together. 'Right, we know we can go any speed, whatever turns up. Row very clean, quick catch, quick legs, get them absolutely spot on, put the message out ... five seconds ... Okay.'
>
> Five seconds was the winning margin of their Olympic victory. Steve and Matt have been a pair for five years now and have only ever had three perfect rows: the heat, the semi and the final of the last Olympics. At times like that you just seemed to hit a groove, the stroke rate came, no problem, and it wasn't hard work in the water. It was like the slow-motion experience that some sportsmen talked about. Everything that normally happened so quickly suddenly seemed easier and controlled. Neither of them could say why it was like this one day and not the next. It was something intangible and that was the attraction, striving to recapture the groove they had struck in those Olympics.
>
> (The Sunday Times)

1 How does Steve's memory of his Olympic victory in this passage contrast with the description of training in the earlier extract?
2 How would you expect Steve to feel immediately after the victory? What do you think he might have done later the same day?

5

Listen to the next extract from the article and make notes of the words used to describe Steve's feelings immediately after the victory and later in the day. Can you think of any times in your own life when you have reacted in a similar way?

6

Order the words below to find out what Steven Redgrave told journalists after he won his fourth gold medal at the 1996 Olympics.

> ever   shoot   you   near   If   catch
> a   again,   boat   me   me!

7

Work with a friend. Discuss some of the things you would like to achieve in your own lives, then each write down a definition in exactly twenty-five words of what success means to you.

8

Listen to the poem on the right. How many of the things in your and your partner's definitions of success are also mentioned in the poem? In what ways is the theme of the poem similar to the ideas in the extract about Steven Redgrave?

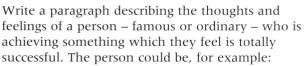

Homework

Write a paragraph describing the thoughts and feelings of a person – famous or ordinary – who is achieving something which they feel is totally successful. The person could be, for example:

– composing or performing a song or a piece of music
– breaking a sports record or scoring a winning goal
– making something with their hands

Call it 'Getting it right'.

What Then?

His chosen comrades thought at school
He must grow a famous man;
He thought the same and lived by rule,
All his twenties crammed with toil;
'What then?' sang Plato's ghost. 'What then?'

Everything he wrote was read,
After certain years he won
Sufficient money for his need,
Friends that have been friends indeed;
'What then?' sang Plato's ghost. 'What then?'

All his happier dreams came true –
A small old house, wife, daughter, son,
Grounds where plum and cabbage grew,
Poets and wits around him drew;
'What then?' sang Plato's ghost. 'What then?'

'The work is done,' grown old he thought,
'According to my boyish plan;
Let the fools rage, I swerved in naught,
Something to perfection brought';
But louder sang that ghost, 'What then?'

W. B. Yeats

Language Summary

Discourse in written text

Prepositions
    Monday morning **in** the Leander gym club.

Fixed phrases
    What then?

see practice page 95

Lesson 3 *Taking flight*

Language focus:	Phrasal verbs related to leaving
	Idioms with *end/last/final*
	Text structure
Skills focus:	Speaking: sharing knowledge and experiences

1

Work in groups of three or four people. Think of:

- four ways to say goodbye in English
- four ways to say goodbye in other languages
- four ways to end a letter
- four song titles to do with leaving or ending
- four phrasal verbs with meanings related to endings or journeys
- four idioms or fixed expressions using the words *end/last/final*

When you have finished, choose one of the categories above. (You don't all have to choose the same category.) Write your four examples in Wing 1 on the butterfly opposite.

2

Work with a partner who was not in your group for Activity 1. Read the quotations opposite and talk about what they mean to you and how they relate to the end of your English course. Then choose one you like and copy it into Wing 2 opposite.

3

Work with a new partner. Choose one of the following topics. Tell your partner about it and explain why it was or is important to you.

- the end of a journey you once made
- the end of a day
- the end of a film or book
- the end of a stage in your life
- the end of a season

Choose up to 25 words to record the story you told your partner. Give your story a title and write it in Wing 3.

4

Work with the whole class. Think of your memories of the class, the people in it, and the things that have happened to you together. Take it in turns to share your memories, each making a sentence beginning 'I'll remember …'. When you have finished, choose three or four of the memories and write them in Wing 4.

Goodbye, goodbye. Parting is such sweet sorrow
That I must say goodnight till it be morrow.
(Shakespeare)

Parting is all we know of heaven
And all we need of hell.
(Emily Dickinson)

Should auld acquaintance be forgot
And never brought to mind
We'll tak a cup o' kindness yet
For auld lang syne.
(Burns)

When you are old and grey and full of sleep
And nodding by the fire, take down this book.
(Yeats)

And the best and the worst is this
That neither is most to blame
If you have forgotten my kisses
And I have forgotten your name.
(Swinburne)

I am a part of all that I have met;
Yet all experience is an arch where through
Gleams that untravelled world …
(Tennyson)

We are such stuff
As dreams are made on, and our little life
Is rounded by a sleep.
(Shakespeare)

5

Work with the whole class. Choose a word or expression related to endings. For example:
The end/Farewell/Keep in touch.
Together, make a poem in which the first letters of each line spell out your word or expression vertically. Copy your class poem into the centre 'body' of the butterfly.

6

Finally, walk round and share what you have written with other people in the class.

Language Summary

Phrasal verbs related to leaving

Idioms with *end/last/final*

Text structure

see practice page 96

Additional material

Answers

1 a) Woman   b) Man   (Marketing studies in Britain and the USA show that men are less likely than women to try out new restaurants or unfamiliar food items)

2 a) Man   b) Woman   (Studies have shown that men unconsciously take up positions which allow them more space in situations like planes and trains)

3 a) Woman   b) Man   (Market research shows that women more often make up their minds about exactly what they want while in the shop, while men decide beforehand)

4 a) Woman   b) Man   (It has been found that women are more likely to savour the chocolate by eating it more slowly, and by finding out what it contains)

5 a) Man   b) Woman   (Some research has suggested that women are better at coping with several different things at the same time, while men prefer to focus on one thing at a time)

6 a) Woman   b) Man   (Surveys show that women are less likely to take the chance of running out of petrol than men, and tend to fill up earlier)

7 a) Man   b) Woman   (Psychologists have found that men are more likely to shop for new things and are more impressed by packaging and claims of new inventions)

8 a) Woman   b) Man   (Men often feel they are supposed to have a good sense of direction and are reluctant to ask for help. A woman may not feel she has her pride to consider and may be more ready to ask for directions)

Unit 8, Lesson 1, Activity 4

Back Scratcher's T-Shirt

* *The fast and logical solution to infernal itching*

The friend (or partner) who offers to scratch your back is a friend indeed. Except it all goes horribly wrong when they just can't seem to locate the maddening itch. For those of you who are fed up of saying, 'left a bit … up a bit … right a bit … oh no!', here's a very special t-shirt, complete with an itch locator grid. You are also equipped with a hand-held miniature corresponding grid-map, for accurate communication. So when the scratcher says, 'I'm scratching F5', you can say, 'try G7'.

Foreign language learners who have tried this Chindogu have noted it's particularly useful for practising the pronunciation of numbers and letters. *"Do you mean G3 or J3?"*

Unit 8, Lesson 3, Activity 5

The Net

Certificate: 12

Release date: October 1995

Columbia

Starring: Sandra Bullock, Jeremy Northam, Dennis Miller

Director: Irwin Winkler

Length: 115 minutes

Rating: ***

Nowadays everyone, everywhere seems to be talking about the Internet. So, it's not that surprising that the Hollywood moguls have jumped in feet first and set a film in the world of the computerfreak.

Star of the moment Sandra Bullock plays Angela Bennett, a hot-shot computer expert, who works freelance from her home. Angela lives an ultra-lonely existence; her only friends are her fellow netheads that she chats to via her computer.

One day, Angela is given a strange piece of software that gives the user access to some top-secret information. Our heroine susses out pretty soon that something pretty weird is going on, but decides that it's not serious enough to stop her from going on her first holiday in ages.

Then, Angela's world becomes a nightmare. First she stumbles into a tall, dark, handsome stranger on a Mexican beach. Which doesn't seem too bad, you might think. Unfortunately Jack Devlin (Jeremy Northam) first seduces her, then tries to kill her.

Luckily Angela manages to escape, but when she gets back to the States, her troubles really begin. Her house has mysteriously been sold, while all computer records of her existence have either been changed or destroyed. Angela tries to tell people her story, but no-one will believe her – especially the police. According to their records, she's a criminal with a history of mental illness.

Not only is Angela homeless, jobless and destitute, she's also still got a killer on her trail.

On paper, *The Net* shouldn't work. Angela's hopeless situation is based largely on the fact that nobody can vouch for her identity. Even if she does work from home and conducts most of her business over the Net, it's pretty difficult to believe that the charming, sassy and pretty Angela really has got no mates whatsoever in the entire world. Also, a lot of the things that happen to our heroine are technically impossible.

However, if you manage to suspend your disbelief on these central points, *The Net* is an enthralling thriller, thanks mainly to yet another utterly engaging performance from Sandra Bullock.

Vocabulary

Idioms with the word *name*

1

Complete the story using the phrases below.

a made something of a name for himself as
b make my name
c name the day
d name your price
e namedropping
f namely
g nickname
h the name of the game
i who had just been named as
j who shall be nameless
k you name it, he'd got it
l your name will be mud

A woman journalist I know, (1) *who shall be nameless*, once got the chance to interview a very rich man called Roland (2) _____ young businessman of the year. He'd also (3) _____ a playboy. Big house, swimming pool, private plane, racehorse – (4) _____. My friend was delighted to have this opportunity – this article could really (5) _____, she thought.

When she was shown into his enormous drawing room she was met by a handsome although rather plump young man, (6) _____, Roland, 'Call me Roller,' he said. 'Roller – rolling in money. Get it?' My friend laughed politely but thought the (7) _____ was quite suitable, given his shape. He was obviously attracted to her, but the more he talked, the more she disliked him. He boasted about his money and his famous friends, he told very unfunny jokes, and he was constantly (8) _____. He also let slip some hints about various slightly illegal ways he'd made his money. 'But this is off the record, you understand,' he said. 'If you print this, (9) _____, my dear.' After a couple of hours, Roland was clearly infatuated with my friend. '(10) _____, my dear, and this could all be yours,' he said, gesturing at his appallingly furnished drawing room. 'No thanks,' she replied, and went home to work on her article.

The next day she got a phone call from Roland, who had come to his senses. 'My dear, you can't possibly want to publish all that nonsense. Let's come to some agreement … just (11) _____ and let's forget all about it.' But she went ahead and wrote the article, which was published in the national press. Roland took the paper to court for libel and, much to everyone's surprise, won the case. The publicity, however, did my friend's career a lot of good – which all goes to show that truth is not necessarily (12) _____.

Language Summary

Newspaper language

Newspaper headlines have their own grammar rules. For example:

1 The articles *the, a* and *an* are often omitted.
2 The number of verb forms used are generally restricted to:
  a past simple – for past time.
  b present simple – for past and present time.
  c infinitive form – for future time.
3 Long sequences of nouns and adjectives are often used.

2

Look at the headlines below and match them to the rules above.

1 100 flee paint factory fire.   *Rules 1, 2b, 3*
2 Return of rich exiles rouses fury. _____
3 Jackpot tops £9.5m for lottery. _____
4 Ticket sales hit all-time low. _____
5 Doctors to boycott gun licensing. _____
6 Car plunge claims 5 young lives. _____
7 Death penalty review. _____
8 Machen thrills home crowd. _____
9 Storms claim more victims. _____
10 Ethiopia halts incursion. _____

3

Find words or expressions in the headlines in Activity 2 which mean:

1 go above a certain level (vb.)   *tops*
2 go below a certain level (vb. + n) _____
3 cause – (a death) (vb.) _____
4 cause – (a feeling) (vb.) _____
5 escape from (vb.) _____
6 please, delight (vb.) _____
7 refuse to take part in (vb.) _____
8 stop (vb.) _____
9 anger (n) _____
10 fall (n) _____

4

Rewrite the headlines in Exercise 2 as complete sentences.

1 *One hundred people have escaped from a fire in a paint factory.*
2 _____
3 _____
4 _____
5 _____
6 _____
7 _____
8 _____
9 _____
10 _____

Language Summary

Reporting colloquial speech

*She said **it would be** quite all right, because the people she was planning to invite were those whom she has known for at least a year and whom she 'knows' as well as any of her other friends that, on the whole, I tend to like.*

This example shows that verbs do not always change to a past form in reported speech. If the situation is still true at the time of reporting, the verbs may stay in the present. The two verbs 'knows' and 'tend' stay in the present form as the relationships are unchanged. 'It will be quite all right' changes to 'would' as the situation has changed – the party has been cancelled.

In addition, what is reported is very often a general summary of what was said, leaving out the 'fillers', repetition and personal references typical of spoken English. So in their conversation, the writer's daughter might actually have said something like this:

'Oh, mum, honestly, it'll be quite all right. I've known them for ages – at least a year. I know them just as well as all my other friends like Barbs and Andy … and Chris … and you like them, don't you? So?'

1

Now report these utterances following the instructions below.

1 (Teacher to class): 'OK, right, now everyone what I'd like you to do next is … are you listening Laila? Just leave that for a minute … what I want you all to do is close your books and find a piece of paper, and write down the numbers 1 – 10, the numbers 1 – 10, OK?'

Report what the teacher asked the class to do. Begin:

The teacher told the class …

2 (Customer to shop assistant): 'Yeah, I bought this walkman here it was er last week, last Friday, and when I got it home it was … I opened the box and the headset wasn't working, it was, look you can see here if you look close, it's broken.'

The shop assistant immediately went to the manager to explain the problem. Report what he told the manager. Begin:

The customer says …'

3 (Witness to policeman): 'I was just standing here and this car came along, it was er, it was white and I'm pretty sure it was a Mercedes, and it was trying to overtake just over there just on the corner and it just got past the truck, the one it was trying to overtake, it just got past it and round the corner and then I heard this great screeching of brakes and a crash.'

Write what the policeman would put in his report. Begin:

The witness said that …

Vocabulary 1

Tend to …

*… her friends, whom on the whole I **tend to** like*
Tend to … is a very common expression in English speech. Its main use is to soften an opinion, or a statement (particularly a negative statement), eg 'I tend to think that the city authorities are generally fairly corrupt.' It is also often used to make a general statement seem a little less certain, eg 'We tend to go to the sea for holidays.'

2

Finish these sentences giving true information about yourself, or giving your own opinions.

1 When I was young, I tended to _____
2 I tend to think that older people _____
3 Most people of my age tend to enjoy _____
4 Foreigners who visit my country tend to _____
5 At weekends, I tend to _____
6 Children tend to _____
7 Politicians tend to _____
8 When I'm angry, I tend to _____

Vocabulary 2

Words referring to insanity

mad, *bad and dangerous*
*an assorted handful of **internuts***
Mad here probably means crazy rather than angry.

Internut is a word the writer has made up by combining *Internet* and *nutter* (see the definition on page 8).

There are a large number of words in English to describe someone who is not sane, or someone whose behaviour is unconventional. Many of these words are highly colloquial, and also very negative, so they need using with care.

3

Sort the words below into three groups:

a standard (appropriate in both speech and writing, in most situations)

b slightly colloquial (used mainly in speech, but appropriate in most contexts)

c highly colloquial (appropriate only in very informal situations)

> barmy   batty   demented   insane   loco
> loony   mad   mentally disturbed   mentally ill
> not in her right mind   nuts   nutty   off his head
> off her rocker   crazy   out of his mind
> not all there   round the bend   unbalanced

Language Summary

Telephone language
*Hi. Thanks for **calling** the Wire.*

1

Complete the script of the recorded telephone message below by choosing appropriate words from the list. You can use some words more than once, and you will not need to use all the words.

call	calling	dial	dialling	enter	entering
hang	hanging	hold	holding	make	making
press	pressing	stand	standing	take	taking

Hi. Thanks for (1) *calling* the Wire, planet Earth's first all Europrogrammed music television network. If you're (2) _____ from a touch-tone telephone, please (3) _____ the line for one moment for further instructions. If you're (4) _____ from a non touch-tone telephone please (5) _____ our helpline 01798 646464 and an operator will be (6) _____ by to (7) _____ your call personally. You may also (8) _____ 01798 646464 if you're experiencing difficulty using your touch-tone telephone. This number may also be used to obtain information regarding video clip selection numbers or an update on our new weekly releases. Touch-tone users may (9) _____ your selection by (10) _____ the three digit code. To correct a dialling error or to change your selection (11) _____ the star button. To ensure your video selection is registered please do not (12) _____ up until the end of this message. Here is the tone. If you don't have a touch-tone telephone please (13) _____ for video selection instructions.

Vocabulary 1

Idioms – *foot* or *feet*?
*I **put my foot down** about that.*

2

Complete the idioms by adding *foot*, or *feet* and then match the beginnings and endings of the sentences.

1 Ken put his *foot* down.
2 They voted with their _____ .
3 He's finding his _____ in the job.
4 He'll _____ the bill.
5 He never puts a _____ wrong.
6 He's got cold _____ about it.
7 Put your best _____ forward.
8 He swept me off my _____ .
9 I really put my _____ in it.
10 I got off on the wrong _____ .

a *Ken put his foot down* when his wife wanted to call their son Cliff.
b _____ – and before I knew it, we were engaged to be married.
c _____ – he's got lots of money.
d _____ – he says he's too scared to do it.
e _____ – I asked her about her wedding and she told me it had been called off!
f _____ – no-one chose to go to the extra classes.
g _____ – the first meeting was a disaster!
h _____ – we've got a long way to walk yet.
i _____ – whatever he does, it's perfect.
j _____ – though the first few weeks have been difficult.

Vocabulary 2

Fixed comparisons (... *like* ...)
*She'd be **gone like a shot**.*

3

Complete the sentences using nouns from the box.

an angel	a bomb	a house on fire	a lead balloon
a light	a log	a shot	a stone	wildfire	the wind

1 He'll be gone like ___ *a shot* ___ .
2 He ran like _____ .
3 The news spread like _____ .
4 The party was a great success – it went like _____ .
5 Drink that, and you'll sleep like _____ .
6 They've never quarrelled – in fact they get on like _____ .
7 The joke went down like _____ – not one person laughed.
8 The ship hit an iceberg and sank like _____ .
9 I took a sleeping pill and in ten minutes I was out like _____ .
10 Her voice is incredible – she sings like _____ .

Language Summary

Imperative + *and /or*

Call *it early in the morning* **and** *you get an apologetic answering machine.*

An imperative followed by ***and/or*** can have a similar meaning to a conditional structure with 'if' (*If you call it early in the morning, you'll get …*). It may be used to express a general fact, as in the example above, but this structure is also often used in speech to express a warning, eg *Do that again* **and** *you'll be in trouble!*

Instead of ***and***, **or** may be used, eg *Don't set off late* **or** *we'll miss the plane.*

1

Rewrite these sentences as in the example.

1 If you keep on working like this, you'll certainly be promoted.

   Keep on working like this and you'll certainly be promoted.

2 If you invest in a lot of new technology, you might end up in debt.

   _____

3 If you get yourself a fax and a pager, you won't need an office.

   _____

4 You'll be in big trouble if you lose that job!

   _____

5 If you forget to phone him tonight, we might lose the order.

   _____

6 If you don't keep up with the latest developments, you'll lose customers.

   _____

Vocabulary

Superordinates

A British consumer **products** *company …*
Superordinates like *products*, *facilities*, *factors* and *features* have a general, summarising meaning. They are often used to refer back or forwards to lists or examples of specific items in a text, eg *The school has purchased a number of cassette recorders and overhead projectors. This* **equipment** *…*

Equipment *such as cassette recorders and overhead projectors should be kept …*

2

Suggest a superordinate term for each of the following.

1 tables, chairs and cupboards   *furniture*

2 silk, cotton and wool   _____

3 malaria, typhoid and polio   _____

4 dishwasher, electric iron, vacuum cleaner _____

5 honesty, intelligence, sense of humour _____

6 height, width and depth   _____

7 newspapers, magazines and books   _____

8 nose, eyes and mouth   _____

3

Add a suitable superordinate from the box below to each sentence. Use each superordinate once only.

areas benefits developments facilities factors features innovations institutions products qualities services skills

1 They manufacture soap, shampoo and toothpaste. These _____*products*_____ are then exported …

2 _____ such as electricity and water are provided.

3 The school has a computer room, swimming pool and gymnasium. These _____ are available to all students.

4 The land is mountainous, with many rivers and valleys. These natural _____ make transport difficult.

5 _____ such as the increase in traffic and the growth of pedestrian areas have changed the town greatly.

6 Dealing with people, dealing with numbers and keeping accurate records are all important _____ required for this post.

7 These new protein substitutes and genetically engineered fruit and vegetables are _____ which many people still refuse to accept.

8 Accuracy, tidiness and attention to detail are all _____ where she could improve her work.

9 His most impressive _____ were his patience, creativity and tolerance.

10 Increased safety and lack of side effects are _____ which make this drug extremely popular.

11 Banks, universities and churches are all _____ which have been affected by social changes.

12 Health is affected by a number of _____ including physical activity, social circumstances and personal attitudes.

Language Summary 1

Verb forms and future meaning

The following verb forms are among those used to express future meaning in English:

1 Present continuous for personal arrangements and plans.

2 *Be going to* + infinitive to express a prediction based on present evidence or prearranged plans.

3 *Will* for prediction about a future event.

4 Present simple for a definite, scheduled event.

5 The first conditional for a prediction the speaker feels is likely to come true.

6 Future perfect for a prediction about an event that will take place before a specified time in the future.

7 Future in the past for a past intention that was or is unlikely to be fulfilled.

1

Match the descriptions above to the examples below.

a I was going to do some sport.   `7`

b It starts at 9.00.   ☐

c If you give the calculations to Jenny you'll save a lot of time.   ☐

d I'm never going to get them finished in time.   ☐

e She'll have finished them before you know it.   ☐

f It'll be a complete disaster.   ☐

g I'm getting the train to the seminar on Saturday.   ☐

2

1 In which of the above sentences could *will* be used without changing the meaning?

2 In which sentences could *going to* be used without changing the meaning?

3 In which sentences (other than g) could a present continuous verb form be used without changing the meaning?

Language Summary 2

Expressing purpose

In order to plan ahead, you need to set goals.
Keep a time log **so that** *you can find out where your time actually goes.*

Both these statements answer the question *Why?*

With a non finite clause of purpose, eg *To/So as to/In order to plan ahead,* the infinitive form is used. For negatives, *not* is added.

With finite clauses of purpose, a subject and verb must be used, eg *… so (that) you can find out where your time goes.*

This type of clause **must** be used if the subject of the clause of purpose is different from the main clause, eg *You should learn how to delegate so that **other people** can do some of the work.*

3

Complete the sentences below using your own ideas.

1 I made a list so that *I wouldn't forget anything.*

2 He finished the report first so that _____

3 You could ask someone else to do it so as _____

4 I helped my friend with her work so that _____

5 I wanted to finish my essay before 6.00 in order _____

6 You'd better set off now so as not _____

7 In order _____, you had better wear formal clothes.

Vocabulary

Fixed phrases with *time*

4

Use words from the box to complete the phrases below.

about	ahead	being	big	nick	play
present	sign	tell	tide	upon	whale

1 I don't like violence but I'm afraid it's a ____*sign*____ of the times.

2 You're _____ of your time with that idea.

3 So there you are – and _____ time too. I thought you were lost.

4 There's no need to _____ for time – get it finished now.

5 Well, I think it's a bad idea – but time will _____

6 She's working in a supermarket for the time _____.

7 They had a _____ of a time at the party.

8 He really hit the _____ time when his book became a bestseller.

9 Help arrived just in the _____ of time.

10 Let's do it now – there's no time like the _____.

11 Now, time for a story. Once _____ a time …

12 Time and _____ wait for no man.

5

Which of the phrases above means:

a The future will show whether something is true/correct or not.

b To enjoy something very much.

c To be successful – usually in financial terms.

d To try to make something happen more slowly.

e Only just in time.

Language Summary

No and *not*

No, I can't!
Don't hum or haw.
It's **not** possible.

No is used:

a To make a negative reply to a question or a request, and to contradict a statement made by someone else.

b To make a negative statement. In this case it can be used in front of a noun or adjective, and means *not a* or *not any*. (Notice that 'no' replaces the article. *It's no secret.*)

c With the *-ing* form of a verb – NO SMOKING

Not is used to make a negative statement. It may occur with any part of speech.

It's **not** possible.
Not all the money …
Not because he is the President …

1

Look at the following pairs of sentences. Which pairs of sentences have similar meanings, and which mean something different?

1 No errors were found.
  They didn't find any errors.

2 He's no teacher.
  He's not a teacher.

3 He was no better.
  He wasn't better.

4 You should take no more than 5 items.
  You shouldn't take more than 5 items.

5 It's of no importance.
  It's not important.

6 It's no secret.
  It's not a secret.

Vocabulary

Body language 1: Literal expressions

Shake your head when you say no …

Body language 2: Metaphorical expressions

Don't hum or haw

2

Add an appropriate verb to each expression to give it the meaning shown in brackets.

1	*twiddle* your thumbs	(you're bored)
2	_____ your eyebrows	(surprise)
3	_____ your shoulders	(you don't care)
4	_____ your head	(you agree)
5	_____ your head	(you disagree)
6	_____ your foot	(you're cross – esp. a child)
7	_____ your fists	(aggression)
8	_____ your nails	(you're nervous)

Do you have similar expressions in your language? Do the gestures mean the same?

3

Match the expressions to the explanations.

1 stick your neck out
2 keep a low profile
3 put your foot in it
4 have a hand in it
5 have a nose for something
6 can't make head or tail of it
7 keep your chin up
8 set your heart on
9 get something off your chest
10 pull somebody's leg
11 keep your finger on the pulse
12 be wet behind the ears

a have an instinctive understanding
b be involved in something
c try to be inconspicuous
d not understand at all
e take a risk
f really want something
g talk about something that has been worrying you
h be inexperienced
i make an embarrassing statement
j stay cheerful
k tease somebody
l know all about recent changes and developments

Language Summary 1

Inversion in conditional clauses

… **should they suspect** *that your marriage is not legitimate, you qualify for immediate deportation.*
… **had this been** *someone I loved, I wouldn't …*
In formal and literary styles, *if* can be omitted and the auxiliary verb put before the subject. This often happens with *should*, usually with rules and regulations, and with *had* in a past tense narrative.

1

Read the information about entry into Kenya, and the problems one tourist had. Rephrase the information in sentences beginning with *should* or *had*.

1 The currency exchanges at Nairobi airport offer a 24-hour service.
   Should you need to change money, the currency exchanges at the airport offer a 24-hour service.

2 For arrivals without health certificates, a vaccination service is available in the arrivals building.

3 Arrivals from regions where there is cholera should bring evidence of recent inoculation.

4 The woman from England who had no vaccination certificate for yellow fever was stopped at immigration.

5 No visitor is permitted to take up work in Kenya without the authority of the Principal Immigration Officer.

6 Drivers without international driving licences can get their domestic licences endorsed in Nairobi.

7 The tourist detained in Kenya had taken photos of the President. She didn't realise that this was disrespectful.

Language Summary 2

What if …?

What if we were *found out?*
What if I met *someone else after the wedding?*
What if can be used to talk about fears. The verb which follows can be present or past; a past form makes the sentence less definite.

What if can be replaced by *suppose* or *supposing*.

2

Imagine you are travelling alone by plane for the first time. Note down some of the fears you might have before you set off.

1 *What if I get lost in the airport?*

Vocabulary 1

Get

In an effort to **get** *round the stringent regulations …*
I thought I'd **got** *to know him quite well …*
If we **got** *married, I could …*
As the day approached, I began to **get** *nervous.*
Get is one of the commonest words in English. Although sometimes avoided in very formal English, it is generally correct and natural in most spoken and written styles. The basic meaning of the word is either 'come to have' or 'come to be' but the meaning largely depends on the word which follows it.

3

Choose phrases from the box and put them into the correct forms to complete the paragraph below.

| get a letter | get going | get invited | get ready |
| get somewhere | get talking | get to speak | get together |

When I first (1) _____ to that woman, I never would have believed I was talking to my future wife. I saw her several times after that first meeting but I (2) _____ to her again properly until I (3) _____ to a dinner party which she was also invited to. After that I (4) _____ from her, suggesting that we (5) _____ for dinner one evening and that's when things really (6) _____. Now I come to think about it, since I've met her, I've taken a lot of trouble (7) _____ for dinner with her and dress with a bit more care than usual. Perhaps I've had a feeling in my bones all along that I might (8) _____!

Vocabulary 2

Documents

… the cherished **document** *…*

4

Look at the words below. Which document or documents might you get when you:

1 get married?   4 leave a job?
2 pass an exam?   5 buy a shirt?
3 finish a course?   6 buy an electrical item?

a certificate **b** diploma **c** guarantee **d** licence
e receipt **f** reference **g** report **h** testimonial

5

Now decide which word from the list in exercise 4 collocates with *birth, driving, residence, school, death, work, firearms.*

Language Summary 1

Linking adjectives together

... *Khazizian is an* **affable and amusing** *guest.*
his **regal, beaky** *features* ...
the same **smooth, suave** *face* ...

When two adjectives are used together, they can be linked in different ways.

1 After a verb: two adjectives are usually linked with *and*.

2 Before a noun:

• when the two adjectives describe different parts of the same thing *and* is used: *a red and green skirt*

• when the two adjectives give different types of information *and* is also used, eg *an informative and thought-provoking talk.*

• when the two adjectives describe the same type of thing either *and* or a comma can be used, eg *an affable and amusing guest/an affable, amusing guest*

• when the two adjectives describe completely different aspects of a noun there may be neither *and* nor a comma.

1

Add the adjectives in brackets to the sentences below. Link them with *and* or a comma where necessary.

1 Monsieur Claude looks ___*calm and confident*___ as he walks into events uninvited. (calm/confident)

2 Among other events he has gatecrashed _____ lunches. (high-powered/political)

3 His _____ accessories have become his trademark. (red/white)

4 He has a collection of _____ suits. (well-cut/linen)

5 Monsieur Claude sees gatecrashing as a _____ issue. (social/political)

6 Simone Khazizian doesn't apologise for her husband's _____ behaviour. (unusual/eccentric)

Language Summary 2

Compound adjectives

No **gilt-edged** *card* ...
his expensive **double-breasted** *charcoal jacket* ...
well-oiled *charm*

Often two or more words can be joined, usually with a hyphen, to make compound adjectives. These adjectives may be qualitative, classifying or colour.

2

Match the words in the box to the endings below.

1 -headed _____

2 -hearted _____

3 -minded _____

4 -tempered ___*bad-tempered, hot-tempered*___

5 -blooded _____

bad	big	blue	cold	even	good	hard
hot	kind	level	muddle	narrow	open	
short	small	strong	tender	warm	wrong	

3

Divide the following compound adjectives into those that describe physical appearance and those that describe character.

good-looking clean-shaven grey-haired middle-aged big-headed well-behaved smooth-talking blue-blooded stuck-up two-faced well-known

1 Physical appearance: *good-looking*

2 Character:

Which of these adjectives apply to Monsieur Claude?

Vocabulary

Synonyms

... *he has been* **pictured** ...
... *he was* **snapped** ...
... *he was* **caught on camera** ...
... *his face was* **seen** ...

Often several synonymous expressions can be used for the same word, in this case *photographed*.

4

Think of as many synonyms for the underlined words as possible. What effect does the change of word have on the rest of the sentence?

1 Monsieur Claude likes <u>attending</u> the main social events each year.

2 He <u>has managed to</u> slip through cracks in security at many events.

3 Khazizian's two children <u>regard</u> his behaviour as nutty and unnecessarily provocative.

Clauses with present participles

But, **having 15 cards in all***, I was not exactly sure which had been stolen …*

I also called my parking garage, **leaving instructions** *that under no circumstances should anyone but me be allowed to claim my car.*

Clauses containing the present participle can be used to express reason, condition, result or time relations (see Unit 4, Lesson 3 for more on time relations). They are used when the idea being expressed is so clear that no conjunction is needed to indicate it.

Present participle clauses can be made with verbs that are not usually used in continuous verb forms, like *have*, *be*, *wish* and *know*. In these cases the participle clause expresses reason or cause.

1

Combine the two sentences below, using a present participle clause.

1 Phone cards are very easy to use. They are often a soft target for thieves.

Being very easy to use, phone cards are often a soft target for thieves.

2 Marcia did not have a credit card registry service. She had to notify all the credit card companies of her loss herself.

3 Marcia knew the thief probably had her keys. She had the locks of her apartment changed immediately.

4 Marcia didn't believe the man who phoned from the bank. She didn't tell him her PIN.

5 Marcia heard that someone had taken on her complete identity. She began to feel that she would never beat the thief.

6 Marcia had messages from store detectives. The detectives praised her ingenuity.

British and American English: Spelling and vocabulary

cheques	*checks*
licence	*license*

The ending *-ence* in British English is usually *-ense* in American English eg *licence/license, defence/defense*

The regular past tense of words like *cancel*, *travel* has double 'l' in British English and single 'l' in American English, eg *cancelled/canceled*.

Words ending *-our* in British English usually end *-or* in American English, eg *colour/color*.

Words ending *-re* in British English are usually spelt *-er* in American English, eg *centre/center*

Words which end *-ise* or *-ize* in British English are usually only spelt with *-ize* in American English, eg *organise/organize*

Other words have different forms, eg *cheques/checks, jewellery/jewelry*.

Some items of vocabulary are completely different in British and American English.

flat	*apartment*
shops	*stores*
underground	*subway*
diary	*datebook*
car park	*parking garage*

2

Make changes to the passage below so that it would appear natural in British English.

I was standing on the sidewalk, trying to hail a cab to get back to my apartment when the thief walked past me for the first time. He must have noticed that my purse was so full that things were falling out all over the place: my checkbook, keys, candy, even a spare diaper for the baby. I fumbled with the zipper but already the thief had returned, bumped into me, and slipped the strap off my shoulder. It all happened so quickly I didn't even really realize what he was doing. I stood there feeling mad with the man and at the same time rather dumb. A cab drew up but I waved it on as I hadn't a buck to pay the driver!

Describing how much money someone has

3

All the sentences below contain expressions which indicate how much money a person has. Complete the sentences with a word from the box.

loaded	skint	rolling	breadline	ends	millions

1 I'm sure he'll offer to pay the bill, he's _____ in it.

2 She owns several large houses and a successful company. She's worth _____.

3 Don't rely on him to pay for anything, he's always _____.

4 We've been struggling to make _____ meet ever since my husband lost his job.

5 Don't worry! He can afford it – he's _____.

6 There's a lot of poverty here. A high percentage of the population are living on the _____.

Language Summary

Describing colours

*the **greenish-blue** shadows*
nut-brown**, **chocolate brown
beige**, **bronze**, **tan

When describing exact shades of colours, we can:

1 add the suffix *-ish* to a primary colour to suggest the colour is similar, but not exactly the same as a primary colour. (eg *greenish*)

2 combine two colours with a hyphen, often adding *-ish* or *-y* to the first colour to describe a mixture of two primary colours. (eg *greenish-blue/greeny-blue*)

3 use an appropriate noun in front of the colour. (eg *nut-brown*)

4 use a specialised colour term (eg *a chrome background*)

1 and 2 are rather informal, and are more often used in speech, while 3 and 4 are more formal and specialised.

1

Choose words from the box to complete the colour compounds below. You will not need to use all the words.

apricot blood bottle cream chrome crimson
emerald ivory jet lemon lime off olive
royal scarlet sky snow turquoise

 jet -black

_____ -blue   _____ -blue

_____ -green   _____ -green   _____ -green   _____ -green

_____ -red

_____ -white   _____ -white

_____ -yellow

2

Now decide which of the remaining words in the box in Activity 1 (which are all specialised colour terms) is closest to each of the colours on the right.

Specialised colour term	Colour closest to the specialised colour term
apricot	orange
_____	red
_____	red
_____	yellow
_____	green/blue
_____	white
_____	white

3

Think of something which is:

1 reddish _____

2 purplish-brown _____

3 brownish-black _____

4 yellowy-green _____

5 whitish _____

Vocabulary

Literary language

4

This is an extract from a novel by Somerset Maugham which is loosely based on the life of Paul Gauguin, the French artist whose pictures are shown on page 25. It describes the time the artist spent in Tahiti with Ata, who was the model for **many of his paintings. Read the text and think of words to fill the gaps. Then look at the box below and fit the author's words into the text.**

The next three years were the happiest of his life. Ata's house (1) _____stood_____ about eight kilometres from the road that (2) _____ around the island of Tahiti, and you went to it along a (3) _____ pathway shaded by the (4) _____ trees of the tropics. It was a bungalow of (5) _____ wood, consisting of two small rooms, and outside was a small (6) _____ that served as a kitchen. There was no furniture except the mats they used as (7) _____ and a rocking-chair, which stood on the (8) _____. Bananas with their great (9) _____ leaves grew close up to the house. There was a tree just behind which (10) _____ avocado pears, and all around were the coconuts which gave the land its revenue. A mango grew in front of the house, and at the edge of the clearing, were two tall trees (11) _____ with red blossom that (12) _____ the gold of the coconuts with their (13) _____ flowers. Up in the mountains were wild orange trees, and now and then Ata would go with two or three women from the village and return laden with the sweet, green (14) _____ fruit. Then the coconuts would be (15) _____ for picking and her cousins would (16) _____ up the trees and throw down the big ripe nuts. Sometimes there would be a (17) _____ in the neighbourhood and a pig would be killed. Then they would go and (18) _____ the meat, and dance, and sing hymns.

(The Moon and Sixpence)

beds bore challenged feast laden luscious
luxuriant ragged ripe runs share scarlet shed
stood swarm unpainted veranda winding

Language Summary

Lists in written text

*… suitable for **dressing, plaiting and ornamentation** …*
*… men and women spend a remarkable amount of time … **curling it and straightening it, plaiting it and bunching it, shaving it off and plastering it with mud, and even sacrificing it** on altars.*

Lists may consist of single words, short phrases or longer, more complex expressions.

For most lists the usual pattern is '——, —— and ——', as in the first example.

The second example is similar but items are arranged in pairs within the list.

In each case notice that the last item in the list is stressed by being different in form from the others (examples 1 and 2) and/or by the meaning carried by the words used (example 2).

1

Complete the following sentences by adding more items to each list. Be careful to retain the grammatical pattern suggested by the first item.

1 A uniform may be a sign of a community, as in a school; of a closed group, as in _the army_; or of a _religious belief_, as in a priest's clothing.

2 Shouting, _____ and _____, the children ran out of school.

3 It was a wonderful wedding. The guests sang and danced, _____ and _____, and finally _____.

4 Limping, _____ and _____, the soldiers dragged themselves home from the battle.

5 The economy may be affected by bad harvests, as in the late 1980s; by _____, as in _____; or by _____.

6 They cleaned it and polished it, _____ and _____, and even _____.

Vocabulary 1

Hairstyles

2

Look at the list of words and expressions. Group them according to the following categories:

a how much hair someone has

b hairstyle

c hair colour

d hair condition

1	a bit thin on top	9	receding a bit
2	a bob	10	shaved
3	a fringe	11	short back and sides
4	a parting	12	sleek and shiny
5	split ends	13	streaks
6	highlights	14	tied back
7	wavy	15	greasy
8	plaits		

Vocabulary 2

Idioms with *hair*

3

Complete the sentences by adding a word from the box.

get	keep	let	place	split	stand	tear	turn

1 I'll tell you a story that will make your hair ___stand___ on end.

2 Look, it doesn't really matter whether it's 30 cents or 35 cents – let's not _____ hairs.

3 When I finish work at the end of the week I like to really _____ my hair down.

4 Their children are always clean and tidy with not a hair out of _____.

5 I don't like having kids around when I'm working – they really _____ in my hair.

6 _____ your hair on – there's no need to lose your temper.

7 The tiger leapt at him – but he didn't _____ a hair.

8 There's no need to _____ your hair out – it's not such a problem.

Pronunciation

Stress and intonation

4

Practise reading the passage with the stress and intonation pattern shown.

The **hair**, || in comparison with every **oth**er part of the body, || has extravagant powers of **growth**. || This in it**self** is sufficient || to make it an im**por**tant symbol || of **pow**er and vit**al**ity || in many **cul**tures.

Language Summary

Clauses with present participle

*One listener agrees, **citing** opinion surveys.*
*Another disagrees, **asserting** 'I don't think that is true.'*
*The other wanders round ... **looking** at everything.*

The part of the sentence containing the present participle is the non-finite clause – it does not have a subject or a main verb. The non-finite clauses in these sentences are similar to relative clauses, for example, we could say *One listener, **who cites** opinion surveys, agrees.* but unlike relative clauses the non-finite clause can go before, after or in the middle of the main clause.

eg ***Citing opinion surveys**, one listener agrees. One listener, **citing opinion surveys**, agrees.*

The present participle can describe an event which happens at the same time as the main verb, as in the examples above, or one which happens immediately before.

eg ***Braking hard**, he screeched the car to a halt.*

1

Change these sentences to include a non-finite clause with a present participle.

1   The committee spokesperson returned to the original topic and said they should support the anti-nuclear campaign.
Returning to the original topic, the committee spokesperson said they should support the anti-nuclear campaign.

2   One person disagreed and said it was impossible to change society.
One person _____.

_____

3   Another person supported him. She claimed all previous efforts had failed.
Another person _____

_____

4   The original speaker shouted 'You're all wrong,' and stormed out of the room.

_____ , the original speaker stormed out of the room.

5   The chairperson sighed deeply and said, 'I declare the meeting adjourned.'

_____

_____

6   The committee members, who all felt rather disillusioned, decided to abandon the campaign.

_____

_____

Vocabulary 1

Gender
*... instead of **mankind**, use **people** ...*

2

Rewrite the following sentences replacing gender-specific words with more neutral terms wherever possible.

1   If you see anyone behaving suspiciously you should contact a policeman.

2   If you need any help a salesgirl will be available to help you.

3   Miss Knott is headmistress of a large school.

4   Sally wants to be a firewoman when she grows up.

5   The increased popularity of convenience foods has led to higher bills for housewives.

6   Man-made fabrics have led to the development of new weaving and dyeing processes.

7   A new uniform is being designed for air hostesses.

8   They believe that man is the only living creature capable of using speech creatively.

Vocabulary 2

Fixed order idioms

A number of expressions contain two nouns which come in a fixed order. It would be totally unnatural to change the order of the nouns, even though the meaning would not be affected, eg *man and wife*.

3

Decide on the correct order for the two nouns in each phrase and complete the expression, linking the two nouns with *and*.

1   She's always sociable and lively, in fact she's the life/soul of any party.

_____

2   Strong materials like denim can take a lot of wear/tear.

_____

3   Before you make an important decision, you have to think carefully about the cons/pros of the situation.

_____

4   Most companies have good periods and bad patches – they are the ups/downs brought about by unstable markets.

_____

5   My two children are as different as cheese/chalk.

_____

6   It's no good making excuses, I don't want to hear any buts/ifs.

Language Summary

Cleft sentences with *what*

***What** you want **is** children.*

Here the word order puts the emphasis on 'children' at the end of the sentence. The general meaning of the relative *what* is 'the thing that …' or 'the things that …'. *What* is not a relative pronoun here – it does not refer to any preceding noun and it cannot be omitted from the sentence.

In the alternative form ***It's** children **(that)** you want*, the relative pronoun 'that' refers to the noun 'children', which immediately precedes it. Notice that here it is also possible to omit 'that'.

To emphasise that nothing else is wanted or needed you can use 'all that' instead of 'what'. Again, it is possible to omit 'that' – *All (that) she wants is another baby.*

These are all very common structures in spoken English.

1

Make true sentences.

1 What I would really like to do tomorrow is …

2 What this classroom needs is …

3 What I find difficult about English is …

4 What I enjoy about being a student is …

5 What I would prefer to do this weekend is …

6 What I dislike about travelling by bus is …

7 What I want for my birthday is …

8 What most young people dislike is …

2

Complete these sentences with *what* or *that*.

1 *What* he wants for his birthday is a ticket for the concert.

2 It's a ticket for the concert _____ he wants for his birthday.

3 I'd like to tell you the story _____ I heard there.

4 He told me just_____ I wanted to hear.

5 I heard everything _____ the storyteller said.

6 I'd like to know _____ she gave you.

7 She promised to give me all _____ I had asked for.

8 They sang the songs _____ he had composed

Vocabulary

Verbs of movement

*Off went the tortoise and his wife, **crawl, crawl**.*

amble	canter	crawl	creep	gallop	hobble
hop	jump	leap	limp	march	pad	patter
plod	skip	slink	slither	stagger	stalk	stamp
stride	stroll	tiptoe	toddle	totter	trot	waddle

3

Find a word or words from the box which could describe:

1 the movement of snakes _____

2 the movement of horses _____ _____ _____ _____

3 the movement of very young children _____ _____

4 comfortable, unhurried movement of adults _____ _____

5 difficult movement, maybe because of an illness or injury _____ _____ _____ _____

6 movement involving regular steps _____ _____

7 movement with swift, soft steps _____

8 quiet movement _____ _____ _____ _____

9 very big steps _____

10 the movement of ducks _____

11 noisy movement _____

12 movement where one or both feet leave the ground _____ _____ _____ _____

Pronunciation

Weak forms

The following words in the script below would be pronounced as weak forms.

the /ðə, ðɪ/; his /hɪz/;   and /ənd/ or /ən/;   he /hɪ/; for /fə/; to /tə/;   them /ðəm/; as /əz/; a /ə/

Linking and elision

Linking: Where two vowel sounds are adjacent they may be linked by a /j/ sound /, eg the /j/ earth

Elision: When clusters of consonants occur together, some consonants may not be pronounced, eg an(d) shines

4

Look at the marking of weak forms, linking and elision in the passage below. Then practise reading the story aloud.

The Egyptian legend of Ra

Ev(e)ry day **Ra**, the **Sun** God, rides in his boat a**cross** the blue (ðə) sky /j/,an(d) **shines** upon the /j/ earth. In the /j/ evening he **sinks** (ðɪ) (ðɪ) hi: below, into the /j/ **under**world, and **there wait**ing for him is a **fierce** (ðɪ) an(d) en**orm**ous **snake** called **Ap**ep. Ev(e)ry night Apep **coils** (h)imself around Ra an(d) his boat an(d) tries to **swal**low them. (tə) (ðəm) There (i)s always a **long struggle**, but Ra is always the **win**ner. (ðə) Each morning, withou(t) fail, he re**turns** as a **gold**en **disc**, shining hi: əz **fresh** an(d) **bright** in the /j/ **eastern** sky. And a **new day** be**gins**. (ən) (ðɪ)

(The Orchard Book of Creation Stories)

Language Summary 1

Present perfect for recent events

Eugenianus **has been revived** …
A sentence of death issued by a long-dead Roman emperor …
has been halted …

To refer to events happening in a period leading up to the present, the present perfect is often the appropriate verb form to use. It suggests that past events, or the effects of those events, are immediately relevant to the present situation. Eugenianus' death sentence is completed history – his reviving to life is what the story is about now.

1

You are one of the doctors caring for Eugenianus. You are explaining the present situation to another doctor. Decide whether the past simple or present perfect would be most appropriate for each sentence and write the verbs in the correct form (they may be active or passive).

a Eugenianus _____ 2000 years ago. (be born)

b His hospital room _____ by candles. (light).

c He _____ married and he _____ a young son. (be, have)

d We _____ him yet that he _____ asleep for 2000 years. (not … tell, be)

e He _____ to death by a Roman emperor. (sentence)

f He _____ to this hospital in Oslo. (bring)

g We _____ a woman, Olava, who can talk to him in Latin. (find)

h Four weeks ago, his body _____ frozen in the ice in Northern Europe. (find)

i We _____ him food like the food he would have eaten in ancient Rome. (give)

Now reorder the sentences and write them out as a connected paragraph.

Language Summary 2

Clauses with past participles

The man **brought from his frozen tomb** *is Lucius Aurelius Eugenianus.*
A sentence of death – **issued by a long-dead Roman emperor** *– has been halted …*

In these examples the non-finite clause begins with a past participle which refers back to the subject of the sentence. The clause may refer to the present or the past – this must be understood from the context – but it always has a passive meaning. Past participle clauses tend to be used more in written English than spoken English.

The man **who has been** *brought from his frozen tomb is Lucius Aurelius Eugenianus.*
A sentence of death **which was** *issued by a long-dead Roman emperor has been halted.*

2

Now complete each sentence by adding a participle phrase.

1 Eugenianus was a Roman gladiator. He was found in the hospital grounds.
The man found in the hospital grounds was Eugenianus, a Roman gladiator.

2 Dr Petrovich was the doctor who was given responsibility for the case.
The doctor _____
was Dr Petrovich.

3 The doctors found a person who could speak Latin to Eugenianus. She was Olava, a Norwegian nun.
The person _____
was Olava, a Norwegian nun.

4 Eugenianus was terrified when someone switched on the electric light. He ran out of his room.
_____, Eugenianus ran out of his room.

5 Eugenianus saw a 'giant spear' in the sky. It was a low-flying plane.
The 'giant spear' _____
was a low-flying plane.

Vocabulary

Collocations
the Arctic ice

3

Match these collocations, which are taken from a description of the plot of the novel 'The Far Arena'. (You will find that various different combinations are possible.)

1 Arctic	**a** doctor
2 oil	**b** body
3 human	**c** arena
4 icebound	**d** warrior
5 frozen	**e** ice
6 brilliant	**f** tomb
7 modern	**g** climax
8 spellbinding	**h** flesh
9 ancient	**i** drill
10 modern	**j** confrontation
11 ultimate	**k** world
12 Roman	**l** technology

4

What can you guess from the expressions above about the plot of the book? Write a brief synopsis of a possible plot, using all the expressions. Start like this: *Deep in the Arctic ice, an oil …*

Pronunciation and spelling 1

Our sounds can get you in a knot

The poem in Lesson 5.3 makes English spelling seem very confusing but actually much of it is quite regular. It is quite easy to predict how to pronounce most English words from their spelling (apart from some proper names). It is rather harder to know how to spell a word from its pronunciation but the number of possibilities is limited.

1

Look at the following words and underline the one in each group with the different vowel sound in the stressed syllable.

1 moon   rude   coup   shoe   chew   you   (foul)   through   two

2 meal   heel   evening   Pete   ceiling   niece   leisure

3 plough   shower   house   ouch!   ow!   low   round

4 heart   part   clerk   calm   laugh   fast   pear   glass   dance

5 son   once   London   on   blood   gloves   brush   sun   tongue   none

6 phoning   coat   bowling   noting   closing   soaring   soul

7 paint   race   say   ache   moustache   lake   grey   eight   April   cape

8 mountaineer   near   beer   hearing   tearing   here   pier

9 height   site   might   ivy   lively   spitting   sty   typing   sighting

10 football   woman   wolf   root   sugar   book   good   soot

2

Look at the spelling rules below. They are all useful, but not invariable guides to English spelling. Find examples of these rules and exceptions to them in Exercise 1.

1 Doubling the vowel makes a long vowel sound.
Examples: *feet, moon* Exception: *foot*

2 Doubling the consonant after a vowel ensures a short sound in the vowel. Examples: _____
Exception: _____

3 Where a word ends with one vowel + a consonant, the vowel is usually short. Examples: _____
Exception: _____

4 Where we have vowel + consonant + *e*, the final *e* is silent, but lengthens the preceding vowel or turns it into a diphthong. Examples: _____
Exception: _____

5 I before E, except after C, when the sound is ee /iː/.
Examples: _____
Exception: _____

Pronunciation

British and American pronunciation

3

Look at the words in phonemic script below. Underline those which show features of British (RP) pronunciation and circle those which show features of American pronunciation.

/nuː/   /həʊm/   /njuː/   /ˈwɜːkɪŋ/

/ˈprɒgres/   /ˈwɜːrkɪŋ/   /kɑːnt/   /kænt/

/ˈlæbretɒrɪ/   /ˈriːsɜːtʃ/   /ˈprɪtɪ/   /bɑːskɪt/

/rɪˈsɜːtʃ/   /ˈprɪdɪ/   /həʊm/   /ˈprəʊgres/

/bæskɪt/   /læbˈɒrətrɪ/   /prəˈfesə/   /prəˈfesər/

Then practise reading the passage below. Firstly with British pronunciation, then with American pronunciation.

The new professor was working late in his laboratory one night doing some research. He was making good progress when he saw a pretty white rat run across the floor. 'I can't let that rat be killed by the lab cat,' he said and took it home in a basket.

Pronunciation and spelling 2

4

The word 'ghoti' was suggested by G. B. Shaw as an alternative spelling for a familiar creature. Can you work out what it is?

Clue 1: Think of the pronunciation of *enough*, *women* and *caution*

Clue 2: It doesn't live on land.

Following Shaw's example, a reader of the periodical 'New Scientist' suggested the spelling 'ghougheighghough' for another familiar word.

Clue 1: Think of *hiccough, jealous, eighth, eight, eighth, though*

Clue 2: It's edible.

Language Summary 1

All, no; both, either, neither; each, every

ironing and **all** that stuff
each one trying to come out on top

Both, either, neither; all, no

Both and *neither* refer to a group of two, and *either* to one of a group of two. *All* suggests a group of three or more. *Both* and *all* are usually followed by a plural noun/verb and *neither* and *no* by a singular.

Each, every

These words both refer to one member of a group but when we use *each* we are thinking more of the individual, while *every* stresses the group membership. They are both followed by a singular noun/verb.

1

Fill in the gaps using *all, no, both, either, neither, each* or *every*.

1 Both Joan Armatrading and Tina Turner have had long and successful careers, but _____ singer has had an easy life.

2 Which of the two recordings should we release? _____ song would probably sell well.

3 _____ celebrity must realise that it will be difficult for them to have a private life.

4 _____ singer will want to have star billing in the show.

5 There is a city called Birmingham in _____ Britain and the USA.

6 _____ singers in the popular music industry must realise that success is unlikely to be easy.

7 The concert is recorded on _____ CD and cassette.

8 At her last concert, the atmosphere was electric: in the final song, almost _____ member of the audience was moved to tears.

9 A single red rose was presented to _____ singer at the end of the concert.

10 _____ member of the audience will ever forget it.

Vocabulary

Describing character

2

The adjectives below can all be used to describe public figures. Divide them into positive (P), negative (N) and neutral (NEU).

> moody rebellious extravagant natural reckless
> immature modest macho aggressive diffident
> unaffected commercialised flamboyant

3

Match the adjectives in Exercise 2 to the following stress patterns.

1 ■ ■
2 ■ ■ ■ ■
3 ■ ■ ■
4 ■ ■ ■
5 ■ ■ ■
6 ■ ■ ■ ■

Language Summary 2

Adverbs and adjectives with the same form

Singing solo
I came in this world all alone …

A **solo** performance (adj.)   I am **alone** (adj.)
She sang **solo** (adv.)   I came **alone** (adv.)

A fairly large group of adverbs have the same form as adjectives. These include:

alone   alike   deep   fast   hard
last   late   next   quick   well

Note that some of these also have an alternative adverb form ending in *-ly*. In this case the meaning may be the same (*Come quick/quickly*) or it may be different (*Hard, hardly, late, lately*).

4

Look at the sentences below and tick the words you think are correct. In some cases both may be correct.

1 Stand as still as you can and breathe a) deep.
                                         b) deeply.

2 She studied a) hard   for her exams so she passed.
               b) hardly

3 Has she worked a) late?
                  b) lately?

4 a) Next,   I would like to introduce our new guest.
  b) Nextly,

5 It's a long way down – hold a) tight!
                               b) tightly!

6 She spoke a) high   of him.
             b) highly

7 I can't sing as a) high   as that!
                   b) highly

8 She a) right   decided that it was a bad idea.
       b) rightly

Language Summary 1

Quantifiers

… **none of** that information
… quite **a number of** corpses
… **a lot of** people
… **one of** the few vehicles
… **most of** it
… **a good deal of** it

Quantifiers tell us about numbers or amounts. They all include the word *of* and are followed by a noun or pronoun. Quantifiers can be divided into four groups.

Group A Quantifiers used with singular, plural or uncountable nouns. This is the largest group. The following verb may be singular or plural depending on the noun used.

Group B Quantifiers used with singular or uncountable nouns. The following verb must be singular.

Group C Quantifiers used only with plural nouns. The following verb may be singular or plural depending on the sense of the quantifier used.

Group D Quantifiers used only with plural or uncountable nouns. The following verb is singular or plural depending on the noun used.

1

Match the sentences below to the four groups of quantifiers above.

1 One of the reports was inaccurate.
  A number of the reports were inaccurate.

2 Plenty of information was inaccurate.
  Plenty of reports were inaccurate.

3 Part of the report/the information was inaccurate.

4 A lot of the report/the information was inaccurate.
  A lot of the reports were inaccurate.

2

Now match the examples at the top of the page to Groups A – D above.

1 _none of that information_ Group D

3

Complete these sentences using *was* or *were*.

1 Several of the reporters _____ injured.

2 A great many of the spectators _____ injured.

3 One of the soldiers _____ killed.

4 Many of the crew _____ left in the hotel.

5 Plenty of medicine _____ left in the hospital.

6 Each of the reports _____ censored.

7 Quantities of time _____ spent in travelling from one area to another.

8 Masses of money _____ spent on sending faxes which never arrived.

Vocabulary

The media

4

Write the words from the box in the appropriate spaces below.

> coverage   attention   cable   campaign   commercial
> empire   exposure   feature   flash   item   live
> local   news (×2)   phone-in   pre-recorded
> reader   roundup   satellite   update

a _cable_ / _____ / _____ / _____ / _____ /
channel

a _____ / _____ / _____ / _____ programme

a news _____ / _____ / _____ / _____ / _____
/ _____

media _____ / _____ / _____ / _____ / _____

Language Summary 2

Talking about specific quantities: Partitives

an **item** of news
sheets of paper

Like quantifiers, partitives are followed by *of*. They allow us to be specific about how much of something we are referring to. They are used with uncountable or plural nouns.

5

Which of the partitives in the box below could replace the underlined words in these sentences?

> bottle   dribble   gang   gram   heap
> item(s)   jug   mound   part   piece(s)
> pinch   section   team   torrent

Choose two alternatives for each underlined word. You can use the same partitive more than once.

1 There's a _carton_ (_bottle_ , _jug_) of milk in the fridge.

2 There was a _pile_ (_____, _____) of dirty clothes on the bathroom floor.

3 It needs a _touch_ (_____, _____) of salt.

5 Several _articles_ (_____, _____) of clothing were found in the abandoned suitcase.

6 A large _segment_ (_____, _____) of the population is living below subsistence level.

7 The public won't be interested in that _bit_ (_____, _____) of news

8 A _group_ (_____, _____) of young men was getting on the plane.

9 She opened the door and saw a _stream_ (_____, _____) of water coming down the stairs.

Language Summary 1

Omissions in colloquial English

Eyes tired? **Switch** *the TV to voice* **and** *it will read messages to you.* *Forget to pack underwear?* **Order** *by 9 PM* **and** *overnight mail will arrive with a new pair …*

The omissions in the first sentences are typical of spoken English. When the topic is clear from the context, the subjects and verbs of sentences may be omitted. 'Are your eyes tired?'

The second sentence is a type of conditional structure. It could be rewritten as, 'If you switch the TV to voice, it will read …' Again the effect is rather colloquial. This structure may be used to give a threat or warning, 'Touch that again, and I'll punish you!' However, this structure may also be used in advertising or promotional contexts as in the text in Lesson 6.3.

1

Change the first sentence to a reduced form, and rewrite the second as an *and* conditional as in the example.

1 Do you need advice? If you write to us, we'll answer all your questions.
   Need advice? Write to us and we'll answer all your questions.

2 Have you lost your credit cards? If you phone this number they'll automatically be cancelled.

3 Are you thinking of doing an English course? If you enrol now you can claim a 20% discount.

4 Have you never been to New York? If you enter this competition you may win a free trip.

5 Are you about to open a bank account? If you bank with us you'll receive a valuable document case absolutely free of charge.

6 Are you being annoyed by large quantities of junk mail? If you write to this address your name will be removed from commercial mailing lists.

2

Rewrite this conversation in its full form.

A Tired?
B Not very. … bit hot though.
A Cold drink?
B Nice idea. Any ice left?
A Might be. Out here or inside?
B Oh, better inside I suppose.

Now rewrite this conversation using shortened forms.

A Have you been to New York?
B I went once – about a year ago.
A Did you like it?
B I loved it!
A Did you stay long?
B I stayed about a month. It wasn't long enough.

Language Summary 2

Noun modifiers

a **movie** channel
an **English-language** channel
a **soap opera** channel

If we want to give more information about a noun, we can precede it by another noun. This preceding noun is normally singular, even if more than one thing is referred to, as in 'a *movie* channel'. This is still the case with most nouns which are always plural when used without a modifier, eg we say *trousers* but a *trouser press*. However, a few nouns remain plural even when used as modifiers, eg *clothes, glasses, jeans*.

The noun modifier may in turn be preceded by an adjective: 'English language channel' – or by another noun: 'soap opera channel'.

For the plural form, usually the final noun is plural (movie *channels*/English language *channels*/soap opera *channels*.)

3

Combine the nouns on the left with the nouns on the right to make compound nouns and then add them to the sentences below. Remember you may need to make the first noun singular.

1	cartoons	a	case
2	trousers	b	sharpener
3	parties	c	games
4	designers	d	pockets
5	clothes	e	channel
6	glasses	f	names
7	scissors	g	jeans
8	celebrities	h	shops

1 Keep your children amused with our 24-hour
   _____cartoon_____ _____channel_____.

2 Entertain with a swing! We offer a full range of entertaining _____ _____.

3 Keep your glasses safe from harm! Buy this leather _____ _____.

4 If your _____ _____ wear out within one year, we'll replace them free.

5 A range of exclusive _____ _____ is found within the hotel complex.

6 Some of the world's most famous _____ _____ have been seen in our night clubs.

7 Special offers on our range of _____ _____ and casual wear.

8 Blades blunt? Can't cut out? You need our new _____ _____.

Language Summary 1

Future in the past

A real life disaster **was about to happen** …
a crash … **was going to happen**.

Structures used to talk about the future can also be used with past verb forms to refer to the future as seen from a point in the past. Although in these examples the crash/disaster actually happened, the implication is often that the expected event (which may have been predicted for a time before or after the present) did not actually happen.

eg *I was expecting to see her yesterday/tomorrow but she cancelled the meeting.*

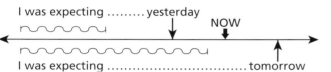

1

Read the diary which gives your plans for Tuesday August 24th. However, on the day you travel something happens to upset your plans and prevents you from going. Write a note to your boss explaining what you were going to do and why you didn't go to Madrid. Begin like this:

'I was planning to …'

TUESDAY AUGUST 24th	
6.30 Taxi to airport	**3.30** Lunch with Trimco General Manager – present details of proposal to him.
8.00 Check in	
9.30 Flight IB615 to Madrid	
12.00 Meet Trimco clients at airport hotel followed by Trimco factory tour	**6.50** Flight Madrid – London

Language Summary 2

Noun and adjective suffixes

*anticipa***tion**	*vision*	*prophe***cy**
*omin***ous**	*promis***ing**	*far-sigh***ted**

Suffixes usually affect the grammatical use of words rather than their meanings. Certain suffixes are typical of nouns (eg *-tion*) while others are characteristic of verbs (eg *-ise*), adverbs (eg *-ly*) or adjectives (eg *-able*).

2

Classify the following endings under the headings Noun endings or Adjective endings.

-able	-al	-ary	-ance	-ant	-ate	-ator
-ence	-er	-ible	-ic	-ity	-ive	-ment
-ness	-or	-orial	-ory	-ship	-ture	-ing

3

Complete the list of related nouns and adjectives.

1 anticipation   **a** *anticipatory*
2 prediction   **b** _____
3 prophecy   **c** _____
4 vision   **d** _____
5 survivor   **e** _____
6 accident   **f** _____
7 _____   **g** foreign
8 explosion   **h** _____
9 _____   **i** empty
10 _____   **j** fragrant

Language Summary 3

Prefixes

*pre***dict**	*fore***warn**	*anti***cipation**	*pro***phecy**

Prefixes affect the meaning of a word and are found at the start of a word. If you recognise prefixes it may help you deduce the meaning of some words. For example, the prefix *pre-* means 'before' or 'in advance', this will help you guess the meaning of words like *predict, precaution, prejudice.*

4

Add a suitable prefix to the endings in the box below and put the completed words into the sentences. Make any necessary adjustments to the spelling.

-stances   -vert   -skilled   -phrase
-millionaire   -colleague   -zero   -social

1 The General Manager of the factory is a very __*antisocial*__ sort of person.

2 They say that to be a politician you need to be an _____.

3 The trip was cancelled due to _____ beyond my control.

4 To my surprise I met an _____ in the airport.

5 It's not usual to have _____ temperatures in Madrid in winter.

6 The factory employs a large number of _____ workers.

7 The manager asked me to _____ one section of the report.

8 If we'd got the contract, I'd be a _____!

Language Summary

Reporting verbs

*… a woman who was **pronounced dead** …*
*Her doctor wrongly **declared** her dead.*
*He **added** 'The family are just extremely grateful …'*

In reported speech, the reporting verb used may give information about the speaker's attitude to the content or about their manner of speaking. In informal spoken reports *say* and *think* are the most common reporting verbs but in more formal texts a much wider variety of reporting verbs is used.

1

Write each verb from the box below next to one of these four categories.

1 Verbs which refer to the volume of speech. *mumble*
2 Verbs which explain the purpose of the utterance.
3 Verbs used for official language.
4 Verbs usually used to describe an animal sound.

> advise   announce   answer   bark   complain
> declare   decree   explain   growl   grumble   grunt
> hiss   inform   mumble   mutter   proclaim   promise
> pronounce   shout   shriek   snarl   state   stipulate
> threaten   wail   warn   whisper   yell

Vocabulary 1

Medical vocabulary

*An emergency **resuscitation** team was called.*

2

Each of the sentences below contains a mistake in the use of medical terminology. Find the mistakes and replace the incorrect word with the most appropriate word from the box. (You will not need to use all the words from the box.)

> breakdown   stroke   keyhole   resuscitated
> allergic   allergy   artificial   bleeding   cared
> crisis   heart   transplant   kidneys   ribs

1 A migraine occurs when a blood vessel in your brain bursts or is blocked.
   A stroke occurs when a blood vessel in your brain bursts or is blocked.

2 She's had trouble with her liver so she has gone into hospital for dialysis.
   _____

3 The main function of the skull, the collar bone and the pelvis is to protect the vital organs of the body.
   _____

4 He had to give up work in the vet's surgery because he was anaesthetic to cat's fur.
   _____

5 Many internal operations are now being done with padlock surgery.
   _____

6 She was rejuvenated by the side of the road at the scene of the accident.
   _____

7 He was prescribed a course of tranquillisers after his nervous crackdown.
   _____

8 The only way to save the child was to give her a bone marrow transfusion.
   _____

Vocabulary 2

Expressions describing state of health

3

Complete the expressions below using the words in the box.

> colour   fit   food   green   pink   rosy   weather

1 _____ around the gills
2 _____-cheeked
3 below par
4 fighting _____
5 groggy
6 in the _____
7 off-_____
8 pale and drawn

9 _____ as a fiddle
10 picture of health
11 down with a bug
12 flourishing
13 in good shape
14 off your _____
15 out of sorts
16 under the _____

Now divide them into those which refer to someone who is well/healthy and those which refer to someone who is ill/unhealthy.

Vocabulary 3

Verbs of voluntary and involuntary activities

*… saw a vein **twitch**.*

4

Tick the verbs which can refer to involuntary actions ie not under conscious control.

blink		burp	☐	cough	☐	flinch	☐
hiccup	☐	quiver	☐	shiver	☐	shudder	☐
sneeze	☐	sniff	☐	stretch	☐	tremble	☐
twitch	☐	wink	☐	yawn	☐		

Language Summary

Expressing general beliefs

People say I'm a masochist.
He is said to have blinded ... over 100,000 men.
General beliefs can be expressed:

1 with an expression such as *People say/claim/assume ...*

2 with a structure containing a passive reporting verb and a *to*-infinitive clause (most commonly *be, have* or a perfect infinitive). eg *He is said to have ...*

 The subject of the reporting verb must be the same as the person or thing involved in the reported opinion.

3 With a passive form of a reporting verb with *it* as the impersonal subject. eg *It is said that ...*

1

Transform the sentences below from the active form to the passive form. Do not change the reporting verb used. Decide whether it is possible to transform the sentence with the forms in both 2 and 3 above.

1 People say that the Korean ghost haunts forests and seashores.
 The Korean ghost is said to haunt forests and seashores.

2 People suggest that the Japanese ghost is male.
 _____

3 People acknowledge the haunting effect of the Jamaican ghost's eyes.
 _____

4 In former times, people believed the English ghost to be a murdered witch.
 _____

5 In Jamaica, people in the last century thought that walking through a churchyard could be dangerous.
 _____

6 People argue that their ghosts are part of tradition.
 _____

7 In many cases people discovered that the story behind the ghosts was part-truth, part-fiction.
 _____

Vocabulary 1

Fear

*... **haunts** the dark **graveyard**.*

2

Write the words below on the vocabulary network and add more of your own.

storms graveyard howl thunder werewolf
scream vault shriek zombie lightning ghoul

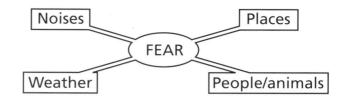

3

Divide the following words and expressions into those which refer to something strange or frightening (A) and someone who is frightened (B).

blood-curdling	☐	petrifying	A
creepy	☐	quaking in your shoes	☐
frightened to death	☐	spooky	☐
grisly	☐	scared out of my wits	☐
my heart was in my mouth	☐	weird	☐
hair-raising	☐	my hair stood on end	☐
in a cold sweat	☐	my legs turned to jelly	☐
my blood ran cold	☐	shaking like a leaf	☐
making your flesh creep	☐		

Vocabulary 2

Enthusiasm

*a self-confessed ghost **freak***
Simon Marsden described himself as a ghost 'freak'. Here, the word 'freak' means someone who is very interested in something; it is a colloquial word suggesting extreme, almost unreasonable enthusiasm. Similar words in English are *devotee* or *aficionado*; these are more formal and can be used for most types of enthusisam.

4

The words in the box below can all be used to describe some kind of enthusiast. Decide which word would make the most likely collocation with the topics listed below. (You can use some words more than once.)

addict	connoisseur	buff	fan	freak

1 football _____
2 films _____
3 TV _____
4 wine _____
5 opera _____
6 computer _____
7 pop music _____

Language Summary 1

Infinitives

*They **must not be sold** even as a joke.*
*You **ought to be doing** the laundry.*
In addition to the present infinitive *(to go, to work)*, there are also continuous, perfect and passive infinitive forms.

a Present continuous infinitive: *(to) be* + present participle

b Perfect infinitive: *(to) have* + past participle

c Perfect/past continuous infinitive: *(to) have been* + present participle

d Present passive infinitive: *(to) be* + past participle

e Perfect/past passive infinitive: *(to) have been* + past participle

1

Complete the sentences below with an infinitive form of the verb in brackets.

1 The washing can ___be___ ___done___ (do) while you're strolling in the park. ☐ *D*

2 You'll find it wonderful to have a machine to _____ _____ (do) the housework for you while you are out having a walk. ☐

3 By the time you get back from your walk the laundry has been washed and rinsed and has only to _____ _____ (dry). ☐

4 I'm sorry not to _____ _____ (locate) the itch for you. ☐

5 One of the partners must _____ _____ (equip) with a small hand-held grid-map. ☐

6 I was meant to _____ _____ (take) a panoramic picture of the view but it would have taken hours. ☐

7 She seems to _____ _____ _____ (try) to get that camera to work all day! ☐

8 The seven pictures appeared to _____ _____ _____ (fix) together in the wrong order. ☐

Match each infinitive form from sentences 1 – 8 above to one of the categories in the Language Summary.

Language Summary 2

Split infinitives

*You must be able **to actually make** a Chindogu.*
Although some people consider it incorrect to form an infinitive with *to* separated from the rest of the infinitive, as in the example above, the structure is actually very common in spoken English. In informal style it is quite acceptable but for formal written style it is best to avoid it where possible by putting the adverb in a different position, eg: *You must actually be able **to make** a Chindogu.*

2

Change these sentences to a more formal style by moving the adverbs so that the infinitives are not split.

1 It's not permitted to even sell a Chindogu as a joke.

_____

2 We tried to really think of a new Chindogu.

_____

3 They told us to carefully read the principles behind Chindogu.

_____

4 I'd like to slowly build up a collection of Chindogu.

_____

5 Chindogu should not be in any way designed to make any comment on the human race.

_____

6 He is thought to generally have been a great Chindogu inventor.

_____

Language Summary 3

Infinitive and *-ing* complements after nouns

*a way **to dry** the washing*
*a way **of keeping** pens from rolling away*
Some nouns are followed by *to* + infinitive while others are followed by *of/for* + *-ing*. These often come in sentences expressing hopes, wishes, intentions or feelings. With a few nouns such as *way*, both constructions are possible.

3

Complete the sentences with *to*, *for* or *of* and the correct form of the verb in brackets.

1 If you feel a need _____ _____ (invent) something just contact the appropriate society.

2 He made the decision _____ _____ (leave) home after the argument with his parents.

3 She had always shown a preference _____ _____ (ride) a horse rather than a bike.

4 The teacher had no wish _____ _____ (embarrass) the student.

5 That student had really no hope _____ _____ (pass) the exam.

6 They had no intention _____ _____ (go) to the party.

7 The thought _____ _____ (lose) him was too much for her to bear.

Language Summary

Complex sentences

The two men, who shared a house in Cambridge … his former flatmate.

In written English, sentences often contain a large number of clauses. Main clauses are linked by coordinating conjunctions, eg *and*, *but*, *or*. Subordinate clauses may be linked to main clauses by subordinating conjunctions, eg *when*, *if*, *who*. Complex sentences may also include phrases with non-finite verbs – infinitives, present and past participles. (See Practice pages for Units 3.2 and 4.3)

1

Reorder the clauses below to make a newspaper account of a road accident in which a famous English film star was involved. The original account had four sentences. You should not add or remove any words.

FILM STAR ESCAPES MOTORWAY PILE-UP

☐	after being involved in a motorway pile-up last night.
☐	as drivers tried to avoid the accident,
☐	as it bolted down the motorway
11	before being stopped.
☐	but three other cars collided
☐	causing minor injuries to some passengers.
☐	Irons, who has starred in many successful films including *The French Lieutenant's Woman*, was travelling with his actress wife Sinead Cusack and their sons
1	Jeremy Irons and his family were recovering from shock yesterday
☐	The family's pony caused further commotion
☐	The family escaped injury
☐	when the horse trailer they were towing overturned on a motorway in South Wales.

(The Evening Standard)

Vocabulary

House and home

*… who shared a **house** in Cambridge …*
*They buy their own **homes**.*

2

Complete the following idioms with the word *house* or *home*.

1 _____ and dry

2 nothing to write _____ about

3 eat someone out of _____ and _____

4 on the _____

5 till the cows come _____

6 get on like a _____ on fire

7 _____ proud

8 a _____-warming party

3

Now use the idioms to complete these sentences.

1 My cousin and I _____ – we're the best of friends.

2 I must say that your family have good appetites, they _____ every time they come.

3 I could listen to him playing the guitar _____.

4 Now that she's passed those exams she's _____.

5 The food was good but the accommodation was _____.

6 At the end of the meal, they offered us a liqueur _____.

7 Now we've settled in, let's invite everyone to _____.

8 Whoever lives here certainly isn't _____ – just look at the mess!

Pronunciation

Homographs

*… had a **row** over the washing up …* / raʊ /
*I can **row** the boat.* / rəʊ /
Homographs (also sometimes known as homonyms) are words which have the same spelling but different pronunciation. They are usually two completely distinct words, rather than two variations of the same word.

4

Complete the sentences below with matching pairs of homographs and practise reading them aloud.

1 They had never-ending ___*rows*___ about who should ___*row*___ the boat.

2 I wanted to _____ that novel tomorrow but then I found I'd already _____ it.

3 The _____ is so strong it'll _____ the clothes round the clothes line.

4 A _____ came to her eye when she saw the _____ in her wedding dress.

5 The nurse _____ the bandage round the _____ on the patient's leg.

6 I don't believe that _____ animals should be made to _____ in cages.

Language Summary 1

Phrasal verbs

*She **wakes up** one day to find all her computer records have been changed.*
*… you **end up** in jail.*
*… nobody can **vouch for** her identity.*
*They have a plot to **take over** the world by logging into the Net …*
Like ordinary verbs, phrasal verbs may be transitive or intransitive and some (eg *wake up*) may be used both transitively and intransitively.

1   Intransitive phrasal verbs, or phrasal verbs used intransitively, do not have an object, eg *end up in jail, wake up one day.*

2   Transitive phrasal verbs have a direct object.

a   In some cases the two parts of the verb cannot be separated. This is when the phrasal verb is actually made up of a verb plus preposition. In this case the object must go **after** the preposition, eg *vouch for her identity* not ~~vouch her identity for.~~

b   In other cases the two parts of the verb can be separated by a noun object. This is when the phrasal verb is actually made up of a verb plus adverb particle. A noun object can then go before or after the particle, eg *take the world over* or *take over the world*. However, if the object is a pronoun then it must go **before** the particle, eg *take it over* not ~~take over it.~~

1

Add the correct preposition or adverb particle to complete the phrasal verbs in the sentences below.

1   No-one wants to come __*across*__ a group of Cyberterrorists.

2   First our heroine stumbles _____ a tall dark stranger.

3   She soon falls _____ the terrorists' hands.

4   The terrorists wipe _____ her entire past life.

5   Our heroine susses _____ pretty soon that something weird is going on.

6   The heroine tries to bring the police _____ to see her side of the story.

7   The terrorists try to warn her _____ but she's persistent.

8   The problem is to prove that the terrorists have made it all _____.

9   The danger is she'll end _____ in jail – or worse.

Match the completed sentences from Activity 1 to the categories 1, 2a and 2b in the Language Summary.

Language Summary 2

Giving more information about adjectives

***pretty** weird*
***utterly** engaging*
The range of submodifiers that can be used depends on the type of adjective, ie whether it is gradable, eg *good, tired, hungry* or expresses a limit, eg *fantastic, exhausted, starving*.

Adjectives which express an extreme or limit are not usually submodified by intensifiers such as *very* or *rather*.

2

Underline the correct intensifiers in the sentences below. In some cases both are possible.

1   When Angela realised the cyberterrorist's intentions she was very/extremely frightened.

2   When the man tried to kill her she was absolutely/very terrified.

3   The police were not terribly/particularly sympathetic.

4   Her situation appeared at one point to be totally/absolutely hopeless.

5   The end of the film was extremely/really exciting.

6   By the end of the film, I was totally/very enthralled.

Vocabulary

Idioms with the word *hot*

*a **hot-shot** computer expert*
Hot-shot is a colloquial term meaning 'successful and confident'. There are several other compounds and idioms which include the word *hot*.

3

Complete the sentences below using the idioms in the box in the correct form.

> be in the hot seat   be hot air   come hot on the heels
> get into hot water   get hot under the collar

1   Every time I try to discuss anything, he _____. (get angry)

2   She's always _____ (getting into trouble). She tells lies and then has to cover up.

3   As owner of the company, you _____. (have to make tough decisions)

4   Although everything he says sounds impressive, all too often it _____. (meaningless statements which sound good)

5   It was an expensive time for him; the wedding of his second son _____ (happened very soon after) his daughter's wedding.

Language Summary

Articles: definite and indefinite

*The temperature drops thirty degrees in four hours, and **the** sea grows as motionless as **a** mirror. **The** clouds and **the** sea now glide together in **a** curtain of heavy grey silk. **The** water grows viscous and tinged with pink, like **a** liqueur of wild berries. **A** blue fog of frost smoke detaches itself from **the** surface of the water and drifts across **the** mirror.*

The is used:

• when we know what the noun refers to from our general knowledge of the world or the situation (*the temperature, **the** sea*).

• when the noun has already been referred to, directly or indirectly (*the water* – which here has the same meaning as *sea*).

• when the noun is made specific by a following phrase (***the** surface of the water*).

A/an or no article is used:

• when a new piece of information is being introduced

• when the item being referred to is a general rather than a specific one:
(the indefinite article *a/an* is used for a singular countable noun, eg *as motionless as **a** mirror,* while no article is used for a plural or uncountable noun, eg *thirty degrees, heavy grey silk*)

1

Complete the text with *a, an, the* or no article.

Out on the safaris I had seen (1) _____*a*_____ herd of buffalo come out of (2) _____ morning mist under (3) _____ copper sky, one by one, as if (4) _____ dark and massive animals with the mighty horizontally swung horns were not approaching, but were being created before my eyes and sent out as they were finished. I had seen (5) _____ herd of (6) _____ elephant travelling through the dense native forest, where (7) _____ sunlight is scattered between the thick creepers in small spots and patches, pacing along as if they had (8) _____ appointment at (9) _____ end of (10) _____ world. I had time after time watched (11) _____ progression across the plain of (12) _____ giraffe, in their queer, vegetative gracefulness, as if it were not (13) _____ herd of animals but (14) _____ family of gigantic, long-stemmed, speckled flowers slowly advancing. I had seen the royal lion, before sunrise, crossing (15) _____ grey plain on his way home from the kill, his face still red up to (16) _____ ears, or during the midday siesta, when he reposed contentedly in (17) _____ midst of his family on (18) _____ short grass and in (19) _____ delicate, spring-like shade of (20) _____ broad acacia trees of his park of Africa.

(Out of Africa)

Vocabulary

Literary language
The sun was driving broad golden spokes through the branches.

2

In the sentences below the original words used by the writers of the texts in Lesson 9.1 have been replaced by more general words, which are underlined. Can you remember the original words used? What did they add to the meaning?

1 The sun <u>made</u> golden <u>rays</u> through the branches …
Original words: drove, spokes
The words stress the force of the sun (drove) and suggest the way the beams radiated out through the trees like the spokes in a bicycle wheel.

2 the light <u>made</u> the faces as red as blood
_____
_____
_____

3 the clouds and sea <u>come</u> together
_____
_____
_____
_____

4 a blue fog of frost <u>comes up</u> from the surface of the water
_____
_____
_____
_____

5 the cold <u>makes</u> a rose garden
_____
_____
_____
_____

6 hot pavements <u>cooled</u> with water
_____
_____
_____
_____

7 the bush <u>goes</u> in <u>low</u> hills to the horizon
_____
_____
_____
_____

8 You <u>go</u> out of the gate into the sea.
_____
_____
_____
_____

Language Summary 1

Position of adverbials

Red Thunder Cloud, …, will be buried in Massachusetts **today**.
He used the language **daily**.
… although only his dog understood him **in the end**.
The dog **always** *seemed to know what he was saying*.
About 100 native American languages are **still** *in use*.
Adverbials can vary in position within a clause, allowing changes in emphasis or focus.

In clauses with more than one adverbial, the usual order is adverb of manner, then adverb of place, then adverb of time.

1

Not all the positions are possible for the adverbials in the sentences below. Circle the number or numbers in the positions that are possible for the adverbial shown in brackets..

1 ¹ Red Thunder Cloud ② spoke to his dog in Catawba ³
(always)

2 ¹ he would say ² his prayers in Catawba ³
(at the end of each day)

3 ¹ his grandfather ² only spoke Catawba ³ (probably)

4 ¹ he died ² at home ³ (peacefully)

5 ¹ did anyone think ² of recording him speaking ³
(at no time)

6 Lenora Penn spent a lot of time with Red Thunder Cloud. ¹ she never ² learnt a word of Catawba ³
(however)

7 ¹ it's unlikely that Catawba will ² be used again ³
(ever)

8 ¹ we should think ² now about the other native American languages and their survival ³ (carefully)

Vocabulary 1

Idioms to do with talking

2

Match the beginnings of the sentences below to their endings.

1 He's got the gift   a his piece.
2 He talks the hind legs   b off his chest.
3 The words stuck   c to keep mum.
4 He said   d of the gab.
5 He couldn't get a word   e in his throat.
6 She promised   f in edgeways.
7 He was struck   g dumb.
8 He got it   h off a donkey.

Now divide the idioms into two groups according to whether they refer to someone who talks/is talking a lot or someone who is quiet/not speaking.

Vocabulary 2

Collocations with the word *language*

3

Think of some more verbs and adjectives that can be used with *language*.

They want to	*preserve* ___ ___ ___	the language.

A language may	*decline* ___ ___ ___	

It's a/an	*minority* ___ ___ ___	language.

It's more appropriate to use	*formal* ___ ___ ___	language.

Language Summary 2

4

Overview of verb forms

Complete the text from the lesson, putting the verb in brackets into an appropriate form.

New York: A senior member of the Catawba tribe has (1) _____ *died* _____ (die), (2) _____ (take) with him the language of his people. Red Thunder Cloud, who was 76, (3) _____ (bury) in Massachusetts today. He (4) _____ (use) the language daily to say his prayers, although only his dog (5) _____ (understand) him in the end. 'The dog always (6) _____ (seem) to know what he (7) _____ (say),' (8) _____ (say) Lenora Penn, his closest friend. Thunder Cloud (9) _____ (learn) Catawba on the knee of his grandfather, Strong Eagle. About 100 native American languages (10) _____ (be) still in use.

Language Summary

Advice

Take great care with ...
It's probably best to ...
You're recommended to ...
Remember that ...
It's usually better to ...
You're expected to be ...
... can be a good idea
... could offend some people
... if possible, avoid ...

Structures for giving advice include:

1 The imperative form
2 *It's* + adjective + *to*
3 Modals
4 Passive verb forms

1

Match the examples above to the four categories above. Then think of two more examples for each category.

Take great care with - 1

2

Complete the text about Bali using suitable forms of the four advice structures above.

(1) _____*Bring*_____ as little as possible is the golden rule of good travelling. (2) _____ leave it behind and have to get a replacement when you're there rather than bring too much and have to lug unwanted items around. You need little more than lightweight clothes – the temperature is uniformly tropical year round so short sleeve shirts or blouses and T shirts (3) _____ . A light sweater, however, (4) _____ for cool evenings and particularly if you're going up into the mountains. Down by the coast a little protection (5) _____ to avoid sunburn. A hat and sunglasses are also useful to ward off the tropical sun. (6) _____ here shorts are not considered polite wear. At some beach resorts they've become part of everyday life but in temples (7) _____ to be properly dressed and shorts don't fulfil that expectation.

Vocabulary 1

Fixed pair expressions

hard and fast rules

Some fixed expressions contain pairs of words which can only be used in one order. These may be adjectives, eg *hard and fast*, verbs, eg *huff and puff* or nouns, eg *bed and breakfast*.

3

Match words from the each column to make similar expressions to those in the examples.

1 bright and	**a** sour
2 fame and	**b** ready
3 give and	**c** pant
4 ifs and	**d** fortune
5 puff and	**e** sound
6 live and	**f** tear
7 rough and	**g** downs
8 safe and	**h** early
9 short and	**i** go
10 sick and	**j** take
11 sweet and	**k** buts
12 touch and	**l** tired
13 ups and	**m** learn
14 wear and	**n** sweet

4

Now decide whether the expression acts as an adjective, a verb or a noun and think of an example sentence for five of them.

That Chinese restaurant does wonderful prawns in sweet and sour sauce.

Vocabulary 2

Words from other languages

5

Choose a word from the box to replace a word or phrase in each of the sentences below.

bikini	bungalow	fete	futon	juggernaut
laissez faire		pyjamas	vice versa	

1 I went out in my night-dress to see what the noise was. _____*pyjamas*_____

2 The beach was packed with women in swimming-costumes. _____

3 The house shook as a huge lorry went past. _____

4 We slept on a sofa bed in their sitting-room. _____

5 They have a small one-storey house on the outskirts of the town. _____

6 There was a village fair on Saturday to raise money for the church. _____

7 The government had a policy of non-interference in private business. _____

8 We help them out with financial problems and they help us too. _____

Language Summary

Verbs with fixed prepositions

*I believe **in** equality …*
*I live **on** $100 a month …*

1

Complete the sentences below with the correct prepositions.

1 James Stone's life-style stems _____ his beliefs in equality.

2 He does not indulge _____ self-pity.

3 His possessions consist only _____ his trailer and its contents.

4 His diet consists mainly _____ fruit and vegetables.

5 He rarely indulges _____ meals out.

6 He does not object _____ other people taking his food and money.

7 He even resorts _____ going through students' rubbish to find clothes to wear.

8 When younger, he would have found it hard to conceive _____ his present lifestyle.

9 He has opted _____ a different sort of lifestyle.

10 His new philosophy springs _____ his beliefs in economic equality.

Vocabulary

Colloquial ways of expressing emotions

*I'm **as happy as a clam**.*

2

The words below are all colloquial ways of expressing happy, sad or surprised feelings. Match them to the pictures.

1   2   3

staggered by …	☐	in the seventh heaven about ☐
bowled over by	☐	miserable as sin ☐
browned off	☐	not a happy bunny ☐
chuffed about	☐	on cloud nine ☐
cut up about	☐	on top of the world ☐
down in the dumps about	☐	over the moon ☐
down in the mouth	☐	sick as a parrot ☐

fed up to the back teeth with	☐	thunderstruck ☐
feeling blue	☐	unable to believe one's eyes ☐
flabbergasted	☐	gobsmacked ☐
walking on air	☐	

Pronunciation and writing

3

Haiku

A haiku is a Japanese name used for a short poem, usually describing a response to a scene in nature. Read the two haiku below. Which of the following emotions do they convey to you?

> regret   happiness   shock

Stretched out on the grass minding my business – this bird, splat! right on my head
Ishikawa Takuboki (translated by Carl Sesar)

Wild geese! I know that they did eat the barley; yet, when they go …
Yasui (translated by Harold Henderson)

Haiku often take one scene from nature and use it to suggest an emotion. Birds, animals, the weather, flowers and trees are often the subjects of haiku. A haiku often consists of three non-rhyming lines, the first usually having five syllables, the second seven syllables, and the third five syllables.

Write a haiku on one of the following emotions.

> happiness   homesickness   astonishment
> hope   sadness   friendship

Choose a natural image related to your own country to express the emotion you choose. Remember that your haiku does not have to rhyme, or follow the same grammatical rules as a normal sentence, but if possible it should have three lines and seventeen syllables.

Language Summary 1

Discourse in written text

Sentences are linked together in connected text by a number of features including pronouns, ellipsis, synonyms, antonyms and linking words.

• Pronouns may refer back to something that has already been mentioned, forwards or outside the text to something understood by writer and reader.

• Ellipsis (omission of words) may occur if it is clear what is being referred to, eg *I was the worst at swimming and she was the best (at swimming).*

• Synonyms and antonyms may be used to avoid repetition of the same word. ·

• Linking words like *However, Although, Because,* etc show the relation of one part of the text to another.

1

Look through the text below and answer the following questions.

a What do the underlined words refer to?

b What are the words that have been omitted at the points marked x?

c Find a synonym for *hit* (hit a groove) in the text and an antonym for *slow-motion experience*.

Five minutes was the winning margin of (1) <u>their</u> Olympic victory at Barcelona. Steve and Matt have been a pair for five years now and x have only ever had three perfect rows; the heat, the semi and the final of those Olympics. At times like (2) <u>that</u> you just seemed to hit a groove, the stroke rate came, no problem, and (3) <u>it</u> wasn't hard work in the water. (4) <u>It</u> was like the slow-motion experience that some sportsmen talked about. Everything that normally happened so quickly suddenly seemed easier and controlled. Neither of (5) <u>them</u> could say why it was like (6) <u>that</u> one day and not the next x. It was something intangible and (7) <u>that</u> was the attraction, striving to recapture the groove they had struck in (8) <u>those</u> Olympics.

Language Summary 2

Prepositions

*Monday morning **in** the Leander club gym.*

2

Read the article opposite, which describes Steven Redgrave's return to Britain after winning his fourth gold medal in the 1996 Olympics, and replace the missing prepositions.

MUM'S THE WORD

Only six people welcome Redgrave home – and they're all from his family.

ATLANTA gold medal rower Steve Redgrave, Britain's most successful Olympian (1) _____ all time, expressed his disappointment today when he returned home (2) _____ a welcome so low key it was hardly there (3) _____ all. As he walked (4) _____ the arrivals lounge at Gatwick last night it was to face a reception, excluding journalists, (5) _____ just six people, all members (6) _____ his family. The razzmatazz laid (7) _____ to greet Britain's sole Olympic gold medallist amounted (8) _____ a single flag draped (9) _____ the barrier. That had been brought (10) _____ his mum and bore the message 'Welcome Home Steven – Our Golden Boy', the letters neatly coloured (11) _____ (12) _____ his children last night. Redgrave's arrival also went unnoticed (13) _____ many fellow passengers. 'I am disappointed (14) _____ the welcome, but frankly I'm not surprised,' he said.

(The Evening Standard)

Do you find the content of the article surprising? Would he have had the same reception in your country?

Vocabulary

Fixed phrases

'What then?' sang Plato's ghost …

3

Match one word from each column to make six more common two-word phrases.

1	what	**a**	way
2	no	**b**	wood
3	how	**c**	then?
4	no	**d**	what?
5	no	**e**	come?
6	so	**f**	problem
7	touch	**g**	chance

Language Summary 1

Phrasal verbs related to leaving

1

How many phrasal verbs can you make using words from the two boxes? Make a list.

be	finish	down
break	shut	off
close	split	out
end		up

2

Use appropriate phrasal verbs from your list to complete the sentences below.

1 If you carry on studying, you'll __end up__ speaking excellent English.

2 You can _____ _____ the last exercise for homework.

3 I _____ _____ the chocolate pudding and then felt sick.

4 They _____ _____ the house and went away on a world tour.

5 They've been married for thirty years – I can't believe they're going to _____ _____.

6 I _____ _____ home now – I'll ring you later.

7 When's the end of term? We _____ _____ on December 15th.

8 The school finally _____ _____ in 1995 as there were not enough children left in the village.

Vocabulary

Idioms with *end/last/final*

3

Complete the idioms and fixed phrases below by adding *end, last* or *final*.

1 … a __final__ reminder for the electricity bill

2 carry on to the bitter _____

3 Famous _____ words

4 He'll come to a sticky _____.

5 He's on his _____ legs.

6 I'm at the _____ of my tether.

7 _____ but not least.

8 It'll _____ in tears.

9 She had the _____ laugh.

10 The judge's decision is _____

4

Which expression from the list in Exercise 3 means:

a worried and feeling things are out of control – unable to carry on | 6 |

b about to collapse | |

c finish something even though it's difficult | |

Language Summary 2

Text structure

5

Here are sentences from the ends of two childrens stories, one traditional (T), and the other a modern version (M). Separate and order the two sets of sentences. Decide which story you prefer and write it out.

1 And Rosamund biffed* him one right back! | |

2 He bent down and kissed her gently, and to his amazement she slowly opened her eyes. | |

3 He parted the curtains and there lying on the bed was the Princess Aurora. | |

4 It was love at first biff. | |

5 On a flower-strewn bed in the castle lay a beautiful prince. | |

6 Rosamund gave him a big smacking kiss. | |

7 The beautiful prince opened his eyes and took a look at Princess Rosamund. | |

8 The King and Queen lived happily ever after too, and the Bad Fairy got even worse. | |

9 The prince's kiss had broken the spell of the wicked fairy. | |

10 The prince looked down at the lovely girl and at once fell in love with her. | |

11 The prince and princess got married and lived happily ever after, and the wicked fairy was never seen again. | |

12 The prince climbed the stairs of the tower and came to a room with a bed hung with white curtains. | |

13 The wicked fairy's spell was broken! | |

14 They biffed happily ever after. | |

15 'Who said you could kiss me?' he cried and he biffed her one, right on her beautiful nose. | |

* thumped

(Traditional story: The Sleeping Beauty)
(Modern story: The Tough Princess)